COOK NOW
EAT LATER

COOK NOW EAT LATER

Mary Berry

Photographs by Peter Cassidy

headline

Recent books by Mary Berry
The New Cook
Mary Berry Cooks Puddings and Desserts
Mary Berry Cooks Cakes
Mary Berry at Home
The Complete Cookbook
The Ultimate Cake Book
Quick and Easy Cake Book
Mary Berry's New Aga Cookbook

First published in 2002
by HEADLINE BOOK PUBLISHING

First published in softback in 2006
by HEADLINE BOOK PUBLISHING

9

Cataloguing in Publication Data is available from the British Library

ISBN 978 0 7553 6314 8

Photographs by Peter Cassidy
Edited by Susan Fleming
Designed by Isobel Gillan
Typeset by Letterpart Limited, Reigate, Surrey
Colour reproduction by Spectrum Colour
Printed and bound by Imago in Singapore

Headline's policy is to use papers that are natural, renewable and recyclable products
and made from wood grown in sustainable forests. The logging and manufacturing processes
are expected to conform to the environmental regulations of the country of origin.

HEADLINE BOOK PUBLISHING
A division of Hodder Headline
338 Euston Road
London NW1 3BH

www.headline.co.uk
www.hodderheadline.com

CONTENTS

Lucy Young and Mary Berry

A DEDICATION
AND SOME THANK YOUS

The book is dedicated to Lucy Young who has worked with me now for twelve years. I cannot imagine there being a day, or my doing a book, without her by my side. She runs my working life, is practical, full of inspirational ideas and what's more, for a trained cook, is a dab hand with computers and disks (something I know nothing about and have no wish to either)! This is the first book we've done by e-mail: for me it usually starts with a large foolscap pad and an awful lot of scrawl. Lucy is definitely a cherished member of the family, and we have such fun working together. She is not my daughter, although everyone thinks she is, but I treat her like my daughter and she treats me like her second mum! Lucy and the rest of my family are trying hard to make me slow down and say no to more cooking commitments and charity demonstrations, and to do fewer Aga Workshop days. But for me it is very difficult to slow down when I just love what I do, and I have the greatest team to help me.

This is the seventh book that Fiona Oyston has helped us with, testing recipes using her meticulous cooking skills. She spent many years as assistant cookery editor with *Good Housekeeping* which, to my mind, has the best cookery department, together with BBC *Good Food Magazine*. I would also like to thank Lucinda Kaizik, who has helped Lucy for nearly two years. She has helped test the recipes in the Aga here at Watercroft, and more often than not goes back home and cooks them in her mum's Aga for supper again!

My cooking certainly has changed over the years. I have to thank our young for keeping me very much in touch: Tom and his darling wife Sarah, and Annabel and Dan. When we've had a day's testing they often take the food home and follow the reheat instructions (as in this book) for supper and tell me honestly how it worked. Annabel, a brilliant cook herself, has contributed too with ideas from her gadding about, many of them vegetarian. And of course I mustn't forget my lovely husband Paul. When I write a book he obviously eats very well for about eighteen months, although anything more ambitious than shepherd's pie or roast beef he tends to call 'mucked-about food'.

I count myself very lucky running my Aga Workshop Cookery School. I am in constant contact with 'punters', many of whom have become great friends over the years. From them I get handwritten recipes on backs of envelopes, and variations on some of my old recipes they have tried, and much encouragement.

And finally I would like to thank all the team at Headline, particularly Heather Holden-Brown for asking me to write the book. That call at 6.15 one Friday evening some eighteen months ago seems an age away now. A huge thank you to the wonderful Celia Kent, our editor, who has masterminded this book from the beginning. It's the second book we have worked together on and again it's been an absolute pleasure. Thanks are due also to the lovely Susan Fleming, who ensured every detail in this book is clear and precise, to Felicity Bryan, my book agent for more years than I can remember, and finally to you, all the readers who have encouraged me over the years with letters of support and photos of your triumphs. I do so hope you enjoy this book, and that it makes your life in the kitchen easier and more hassle free.

INTRODUCTION

This book is all about being organised. It's about preparing and cooking ahead, whether you are feeding the family casually in the kitchen or friends more formally in the dining room. We all love entertaining, but sometimes the reality of the many separate parts involved in a meal can seem daunting. How long will the pudding take to set? When can I prepare the vegetables? Will the potatoes be ready at the same time as the meat? Will the whole house smell of fish when I sear the sea bass skin? When can I talk to my friends if I'm stuck in the kitchen? Panic can set in, but that's where I will come to your rescue.

In a book such as this, where the concept is 'cook now, eat later', it would be easy to give you recipes that could all be cooked completely in advance, and that merely needed reheating. Easy, yes, but a bit boring. What I have done is gather together my very latest, up-to-the-minute recipes, many of which, I will happily admit, need some last-minute attention. But various stages of them can be prepared and/or cooked in advance, which means that on the day itself, you will have much less to do, and will not feel too much under immediate pressure. The recipes themselves are divided into easy-to-follow numbered steps, and that's essentially what I want to do here: help you to be one step ahead of the game.

Being organised so far as food and entertaining are concerned is not just to do with the actual cooking. For instance, if you order the fish or meat you want well in advance from fishmonger, butcher or supermarket, that's one aspect of the meal taken care of. We all think freshly prepared is best, but many vegetables can be peeled, trimmed and cut at least the day before, which means one less chore on the day. And don't ever be ashamed of cutting corners to enable you to be organised and ahead. Buy ready-prepared vegetables or salad leaves in packets if you think you won't have time: they're more expensive, but your peace of mind might be more important than cost. Even counting out the napkins, and checking on candles and cutlery a couple of days in advance, puts you a step or so ahead.

But the majority of the information here does actually concern some degree of cooking, and when you are doing this in advance, there are certain stages which must be followed. The refrigerator is intimately involved in this, and the 'rules' concerning cooling and chilling are particularly important. Make sure your fridge is working properly. The ideal temperature for the short-term storage of perishable foods is just above freezing point. Individual makes of fridges vary, but the temperature range should be between 1° and 7°C (34°–44°F).

Preparing and Cooking Ahead

I won't detail every single way in which you can prepare and cook ahead, but just give you a few general ideas.

Firstly preparation, which does not require cooking. Many non-cooked cold starters and desserts can be completely prepared ahead and stored in the fridge, to set and/or chill. Meats, fish and vegetables can be marinated overnight in the fridge, ready for cooking the next day. Many vegetables can be prepared in advance, and kept raw in the fridge. Savoury butters – handy for so many uses – last well in the fridge, and some uncooked stuffings can be assembled with meats or fish, and carefully chilled until it's time to cook. (Always buy the very finest quality of freshest fish and meat.) Raw pastry, bought or home-made, positively benefits from being kept in the fridge, after rolling and cutting into the desired shapes.

Everything must be carefully covered, to prevent smells permeating where they shouldn't, or surfaces drying. Clingfilm and foil are invaluable tools for those who want to get ahead! Some foods need to breathe when stored, like cheese, which is best wrapped in greaseproof or wax paper.

Cooking ahead perhaps lies at the heart of the book. Many dishes require part-cooking a day or hours before, and then finishing off at the last minute. Some fish, for instance, can be seared briefly to brown the day before, then chilled and baked or grilled for a few minutes before serving. The same can apply to some poultry and game dishes, especially prime cuts such as breasts. Many stew-type dishes and soups can be completely cooked ahead and kept in the fridge for a couple of days – and most of these can be frozen (see below). Root vegetables can be char-grilled ahead then blasted with heat at the last minute.

In general, try to slightly *under*cook things if cooking completely ahead. You will have to reheat until piping hot, and you don't want things to overcook and disintegrate. Even if the main ingredient in a meal cannot be cooked in advance – like roast beef, for instance – you can pre- or part-cook its accompaniments, the Yorkshire puds and the roast potatoes. While the meat is resting, you will have plenty of time to bring them up to crisp, golden perfection.

Suggested cooking times and cooking techniques are given for the Aga at the end of each recipe. When the top of the oven is used, obviously cooking on the Aga hotplates is very similar, and so I haven't gone into too much detail there. But occasionally, instead of cooking on the Simmering Plate and losing heat by keeping the lid up for a long time, you can cover and cook something like onions in the Simmering Oven. Bring a sauce, stew or casserole to the boil on the Boiling Plate then cover, transfer to the Simmering Oven and cook until tender. This means that although they take longer to cook, they will not boil over, they don't need to be watched, and they will be beautifully tender. And, most importantly, the Aga will not lose too much heat through the open lids.

Cooling and Chilling

These are vital elements of preparing and cooking ahead. When you have partially or completely cooked something, you want it to cool as quickly as possible before chilling. The first thing to do is simple: take off the lid! One option with a casserole-type dish is to decant it from its one hot cooking pot into two smaller, cold dishes, or a shallow roasting tray. This means that more area is exposed to cool air, but also means extra washing-up, so I'm not too keen. And I don't think you need to use cold water baths or ice. A cool ambient temperature, such as in a larder or pantry, should be sufficient.

Once a dish is cool, it must then be covered, with a lid, clingfilm or foil, and stored in the fridge for the recommended time.

Efficient cooling and chilling are particularly important when you are cooking for a crowd. Larger quantities of food cooked together, because of their density, will take longer to cool. In this case, you may be obliged to decant them into other dishes (get someone else to do the washing-up!).

And if you haven't room enough in your own fridge, ask your friends and neighbours to lend theirs. It's the least they can do if they're coming to eat your delicious food!

Never add a garnish to a cooked dish before chilling and/or freezing. Do so when it is reheated, immediately before serving.

Freezing and Thawing

The freezer can be used very creatively when you are planning, preparing and cooking ahead. Even if you just use it to freeze basics such as butter or bread, you can be one step ahead, in that you don't have to rush to the shops at the last minute. And blanched home-grown green vegetables can be happily frozen.

If you like to cook things fresh at the last moment, there are a number of dishes here that can be prepared – the *Chilean Chicken* on page 69, for example – and frozen raw. Sauces, stocks and soups can be made and frozen well in advance, as can dishes in sauces, such as casseroles or curries. Baked goods can also be frozen very successfully – a huge advantage when someone phones up to invite themselves to tea!

When freezing, always clearly label the dish with a permanent marker pen – the date, the amount it serves and what it is. There is nothing more annoying than finding food in the freezer you have no idea about! You could also add any useful comment you have room for on the label, such as 'specially good', or 'serve with mash' etc. Freeze soup in meal-sized containers – this avoids having to defrost the whole lot for one person. (Don't add the cream to a soup if you are freezing it: do that when you are reheating.) Freeze stock in old cream or yogurt pots – 300–600ml (½–1 pint) plastic pots – then when the recipe states 600ml (1 pint) it is easy to take out just the required amount from the freezer.

When making a complete dish – lasagne or fish pie, say – freeze raw in the dish you are going to cook it in. If you need the dish while it is in the freezer, thaw it for about an hour, loosen the edges, turn out in one solid lump and put in a bag back in the freezer. The dish can then be used and the frozen lasagne can be put back into the dish when it is free again.

Always thaw in the fridge overnight before cooking, and do not cook something in a dish straight from the freezer or the heat of the oven is likely to crack the dish.

Do remember, though, that some things are just not suitable for the freezer. In each of the recipes throughout the book, I give detailed timing instructions, or warn you against.

Reheating and Refreshing

When a dish is taken straight from the fridge, whether it is fully cooked or partially cooked, it will be cold, and therefore could take slightly longer to cook to piping hot – the desired temperature. Use your judgement, and where useful I have mentioned this in the recipe notes. (Incidentally, a thick dish will need its cooking time extended as well.)

If taking an ovenproof porcelain dish straight from the fridge, remember to let it come to room temperature for a little while before cooking, so that the dish doesn't crack from the shock in the oven.

'Refreshing' is the term used for bringing back to life baked goods in general after they have been chilled or defrosted. Breads always taste better when they are warm, but some muffins and scones can taste like new when reheated. It must not be an extreme heat – you don't want to make many things crisp and dry – but just enough to warm the food through thoroughly.

Those, then, are the 'rules'! Now I hope you will enjoy cooking these recipes as much as we have enjoyed testing them. Remember always that cooking should be fun. If you follow my advice about preparing and cooking ahead, I think you will recognise that that is true. Cooking *is* a true pleasure (so long as you are well organised!), and you will be able to relax and enjoy eating with your friends and family.

SOUPS AND FIRST COURSES

The starter is the first thing your guests will see and sample, so it must look and taste good. I like to arrange my cold starters on the table ready for when we go into the kitchen or dining room. I think it looks so welcoming – and so organised! This is practical as well, because if the starters have been in the fridge, they always need a little time at room temperature: if food is too cold, you can't taste anything. Cold starters are commonly considered to be the most useful for the cook. They need very little last-minute attention, certainly in the way of cooking, and if the dessert is cold as well, it allows you to spend more time and energy on the main course (usually the high point of any meal) and, most important of all, more time with your guests.

However, hot starters should never be ignored, because if you are organised, and prepare the basics well in advance as I advise here, a final quick heat through in the oven or under the grill – which is all most of them need – is easy. And a hot starter, particularly on a cold winter's day, is always welcome. Soups are perhaps the easiest of the lot, as most can be made at least 1 month in advance and frozen. All you need to do is remember to defrost them overnight, or, at a pinch, melt the frozen block gently in a saucepan. (And I think hot plates for soup are vital: warm soup is *not* the same as hot soup.)

Most of the recipes here are simple to make, although some might seem a little more complicated. But as the method is divided up into separate stages you should never find it too much of a chore. Soufflés, for instance, are said to be the bane of most cooks' lives, but mine can be cooked up to 2 days in advance (actually they can even be frozen), and then given a quick blast in a hot oven to puff them up finally.

And don't forget to serve hot bread or rolls with the first course. You can buy some lovely breads now in bakeries and supermarkets, and warming them through makes most taste even better. If you make the rolls on page 186, freeze them in quantities for the number of guests you expect, then simply defrost and heat.

Smoked Haddock Bouillabaisse

Winter Vegetable Soup **V**

The Very Best Porcini Mushroom Soup **V**

Butternut Squash Soup **V**

Fresh Salmon and Dill Terrines

Garlic-stuffed Grilled Mussels

Char-grilled Vegetables with Goat's Cheese **V**

Individual Baked Artichoke and Parma Ham Galettes

Prawn and Avocado Tians

Crab Cakes with Mild Chilli Sauce

Asparagus and Quail's Egg Salad

Twice-baked Tomato and Feta Soufflés **V**

For more starter ideas, see:

Double Haddock and Herb Fish Cakes (see page 39)

Chilled Mediterranean Salad (see page 94)

Herb Falafels (see page 119)

Onion, Apple and Stilton Little Quiches (see page 120)

Roasted Field Mushrooms with Couscous and Feta (see page 124)

Parisian Red Peppers (see page 127)

Turkey Salad with Avocado, Bacon and Pesto Dressing (see page 141)

Peppadew and Chèvre Crostini (see page 252)

Smoked haddock bouillabaisse

A good substantial soup, a meal in itself served with lots of crusty bread and a salad to follow. I have used full-fat milk to give a good creamy flavour. Add a little cream before serving if you use a low-fat milk.

Serves 6

50g (2 oz) butter	40g (1½ oz) plain flour
4–6 spring onions, thinly sliced	600ml (1 pint) fish or vegetable stock
6 celery sticks, sliced	salt and freshly ground black pepper
2 medium carrots, chopped into 1cm (½ in) dice	700g (1½ lb) smoked haddock, skinned and chopped into bite-sized pieces
450g (1 lb) old potatoes, peeled and cut into 2cm (¾ in) chunks	600ml (1 pint) full-fat milk
	chopped fresh dill to garnish

1 Heat the butter in a large pan. Add the prepared spring onions, celery and carrots, stir to coat the vegetables in the butter, then cover and cook gently until beginning to soften. Add the potatoes and cook for a further 1–2 minutes.

2 Add the flour to the vegetables, stir and then add the stock. Add black pepper to taste, but no salt at this stage as the fish is very salty. Bring to the boil and simmer until the vegetables are tender, about 10–15 minutes.

3 Add the haddock and milk to the vegetable mixture in the pan and simmer gently for 5–10 minutes until the fish is cooked.

4 Adjust the seasoning and garnish with dill.

cook now, eat later

TO PREPARE AND COOK AHEAD Complete the soup but don't add the garnish yet. Cool, pour into a suitable container and keep in the fridge for 24 hours. Reheat until piping hot.

TO FREEZE Not suitable.

TO COOK IN THE AGA Start on the Boiling Plate. When the vegetables and stock are added, cover and bring to the boil. Transfer to the Simmering Oven and cook until the vegetables are tender. Add the haddock and milk and simmer on the Simmering Plate for about 5 minutes. Continue with the recipe.

Clockwise from top left: The Very Best Porcini Mushroom Soup; Butternut Squash Soup; Smoked Haddock Bouillabaisse

Winter vegetable soup V

This is a lovely home-made soup, using all vegetables in season, and has been our favourite soup this winter. It is delicious as a first course when there's not much to follow, or for lunch on a cold winter's day. If you are in a hurry, use a food processor to chop the vegetables, but be sure to leave them quite chunky.

Serves 6

50g (2 oz) butter

2 small red onions, finely chopped

2 leeks, finely chopped

3 celery sticks, finely sliced

2 large garlic cloves, crushed

4 level tablespoons plain flour

500ml (18 fl oz) tomato passata

2 large potatoes, peeled and finely diced

1 × 400g can chopped tomatoes

1–2 level tablespoons caster sugar

2 tablespoons tomato purée

1.1 litres (2 pints) chicken or
   vegetable stock

salt and freshly ground black pepper

chopped fresh parsley

1 Melt the butter in a large saucepan and add the onions, leeks, celery and garlic. Stir over a high heat for a few minutes, then lower the heat, cover the pan and cook gently for about 10 minutes to soften.

2 Whisk the flour with a quarter of the passata in a bowl until well blended and smooth. Add the remaining passata.

3 Add the potatoes, tomatoes, sugar and tomato purée to the pan. Blend in the passata and the stock, stir and allow to thicken. Bring to the boil and season. Cover and cook over a gentle heat for about 20–30 minutes or until the vegetables are tender.

4 Check seasoning and serve hot, scattered with plenty of parsley.

cook now, eat later

TO PREPARE AND COOK AHEAD Cool the soup after step 3, cover and store in the fridge for up to 3 days. Bring to the boil and scatter parsley on top to serve.

TO FREEZE Pour the soup into a freezer container, cool, cover and freeze for up to 1 month. Thaw at room temperature for about 8 hours, or overnight in the fridge.

TO COOK IN THE AGA At step 1, cook the vegetables covered in the Simmering Oven for about 10 minutes to soften. Return the pan to the Simmering Oven at step 3, cover and cook for about 15–30 minutes until the vegetables are tender.

The very best porcini mushroom soup ᵛ

Mushroom soup is a classic, but there are very few tasty ones with intense flavour. Older mushrooms will give the soup a better colour and flavour, and they are sometimes sold off more cheaply. You will find it easier to strain off the mushroom and onion into a sieve and just process the vegetables, adding a little of the liquid rather than lots of batches. Return to the pan with the strained liquid.

Serves 6–8

20–25g (¾–1 oz) dried porcini (cep) mushrooms	75ml (⅛ pint) white wine
150ml (¼ pint) water	1.7 litres (3 pints) good chicken, turkey or vegetable stock
40g (1½ oz) butter	salt and freshly ground black pepper
2 large Spanish onions, finely chopped	2 tablespoons dark soy sauce
2 large garlic cloves, crushed	1 teaspoon lemon juice
700g (1½ lb) open mushrooms, roughly sliced	3 tablespoons double cream
75g (3 oz) plain flour	3 tablespoons sherry (optional)
	lots of chopped fresh parsley

1 Soak the porcini mushrooms for 30 minutes in the water.

2 Melt the butter in a deep saucepan, add the onions and fry on a high heat for a few minutes, without colouring. Lower the heat, cover the pan and cook gently for about 10 minutes until the onion is tender. Add the garlic and open mushrooms and fry over a high heat, stirring all the time, for a further 2–3 minutes.

3 Measure the flour, wine and a small amount of cold stock into a bowl and whisk until smooth.

4 Remove the pan from the heat and slowly stir in the flour mixture and the rest of the stock, stirring until well blended and smooth. Bring to the boil for a couple of minutes until thickened, then add the porcini mushrooms and their carefully strained soaking liquid. Season with salt, pepper, soy sauce and lemon juice. Cover and simmer gently for 15–20 minutes.

5 Allow to cool slightly (until safe enough to handle). Transfer to a food processor and blend until smooth. The soup will not be completely smooth, but will still have some texture from the mushrooms.

6 Check the seasoning and stir in the cream and sherry (if using). Garnish generously with chopped parsley, and serve with some warm crusty bread.

recipe continued overleaf

cook now, eat later

> **TO PREPARE AND COOK AHEAD** Before adding the cream or parsley, allow the soup to cool, transfer to a container and keep in the fridge for up to 3 days. Reheat until piping hot, then add the cream and parsley and serve.
>
> **TO FREEZE** Cool, pack and freeze the soup, before adding the parsley or cream, for up to a month. Thaw the soup at room temperature for about 8 hours or overnight in the fridge. Or if you are in a hurry, put the frozen block of soup in a pan over a low heat, stirring!
>
> **TO COOK IN THE AGA** Make the soup in the same way as above, cooking the onion covered in a pan in the Simmering Oven for about 20 minutes in step 2, and 15–20 minutes covered in the Simmering Oven, in step 4.
>
> **TIP** Cep and porcini mushrooms are the same – 'cep' or 'cèpe' is French in origin, and 'porcini' is Italian. They can be found fresh, but are mostly available dried. They add intense flavour to soups and stews, usually soaked for about 20–30 minutes in warm water before cooking. Add the soaking liquid too as this has a wonderfully intense flavour (strain it well to get rid of any grit).

Butternut squash soup ᵛ

Unlike pumpkins, butternut squashes are available all year. Shaped like a large pear, they have a sweet orange flesh. Roasting them first in the oven means that you don't have to tackle removing the tough skin, and it fills the kitchen with a delicious aroma!

Serves 6

3 small butternut squashes, about 1.6kg (3½ lb) total weight	2 large celery sticks, sliced
about 2 tablespoons olive oil	1 × 2.5cm (1 in) piece fresh root ginger, grated
salt and freshly ground black pepper	1.1–1.3 litres (2–2¼ pints) vegetable or chicken stock
freshly grated nutmeg	
25g (1 oz) butter	a sprig of fresh rosemary or 1 teaspoon dried rosemary
1 large onion, roughly chopped	
2 large carrots, roughly chopped	

Preheat the oven to 200°C/400°F/Gas 6.

1 Cut the butternut squashes in half lengthways. Scoop out the seeds with a metal spoon and discard. Arrange the squash halves cut side up in a roasting tin just big enough to hold them in a single layer, and drizzle over the olive oil. Season the squash halves with salt, pepper and nutmeg. Pour 150ml (¼ pint) water around the squash halves. Cook in the preheated oven for about 1¼ hours, basting occasionally, until very tender. Allow to cool.

2 Melt the butter in a large pan and add the onion, carrot, celery and ginger. Cook for 5–10 minutes until beginning to soften. Add the stock, rosemary and seasoning, bring to the boil then partially cover and simmer for about 20 minutes until the vegetables are tender.

3 When cool enough to handle scoop the flesh from the squash halves and add to the pan. Blend the vegetables in a liquidiser or food processor until smooth. (If you use a food processor, it is easier to process the vegetables with a little of the liquid, adding the remaining liquid to the processed vegetables to make the soup.)

4 Taste for seasoning and serve hot with crusty bread.

cook now, eat later

TO PREPARE AND COOK AHEAD Allow to cool, transfer to a suitable container, cover and keep in the fridge for up to 3 days. Reheat thoroughly to serve.

TO FREEZE Cool the soup at the end of step 3. Pack and freeze for up to 3 months. Thaw at room temperature for 8 hours or overnight in the fridge. Reheat thoroughly to serve.

TO COOK IN THE AGA Cook the squash as in step 1 in a roasting tin on the second set of runners in the Roasting Oven for about 1 hour until tender. Cook the first part of step 2 on the Simmering Plate, then add the stock, etc. Bring to the boil on the Boiling Plate for about 4 minutes, cover and transfer to the Simmering Oven for about 20 minutes. Continue with the recipe.

Fresh salmon and dill terrines

These terrines are impressive and very easy to make – no gelatine! Don't expect them to set firm, it is a soft and light consistency. They can be made a day ahead in small round or oval ramekins or indeed avocado dishes at a push.

Serves 6

350g (12 oz) fresh salmon fillet (boned weight)	6 tablespoons full-fat crème fraîche
salt and freshly ground black pepper	2 tablespoons chopped fresh dill
6 small sprigs of fresh dill	juice of ½ lemon
3 slices smoked salmon	
6 tablespoons 'light' low-calorie mayonnaise	TO SERVE
	a few salad leaves, dressed
	6 lemon wedges

Preheat the oven to 160°C/325°F/Gas 3.

1 Season the fresh salmon with salt and pepper and wrap in one layer of buttered foil. Slide on to a baking sheet and bake until just opaque, about 10 minutes. Remove any skin (but keep any juice which has come out of the fish). Allow to cool to lukewarm.

2 Wet the inside of 6 small ramekins and line with clingfilm. Place a sprig of dill in the base of each and cut 6 discs of smoked salmon to fit neatly into the base on top of the dill. (If there is not enough smoked salmon to make 6 complete discs, use the odd pieces to form circles.) Use the base of the ramekin on top of the slice of smoked salmon to judge a circle.

3 Flake the cold salmon fillet, removing any bones. Mix the salmon and any cooked jelly with the mayonnaise and crème fraîche in a bowl, and season with the dill, lemon juice, salt and pepper. Taste and add more seasoning if necessary. Divide evenly between the ramekins and cover with any overhanging clingfilm. Allow to set in the fridge for about 12 hours, preferably overnight.

4 The next day turn out on a few dressed salad leaves. Serve with brown bread and butter.

cook now, eat later

> **TO PREPARE AND COOK AHEAD** Completely make up to 2 days ahead. Keep in the fridge. Turn out up to 2 hours ahead and keep in the fridge until just before serving.
>
> **TO FREEZE** Not suitable.
>
> **TO COOK IN THE AGA** Cook the salmon for about 8 minutes in the Roasting Oven on the lowest set of runners.

Garlic-stuffed grilled mussels

Choose the large, green-lipped New Zealand mussels for this dish. They look stunning and are less fiddly than the normal smaller, blue-grey mussels. They are available pre-cooked from good supermarkets or, of course, you can cook your own.

Serves 6

1kg (2¼ lb) green-lipped New Zealand
   mussels (about 36)
about 50ml (2 fl oz) water or white wine
a knob of butter
1 small onion, finely chopped
2 garlic cloves, crushed
3 fresh tomatoes
about 75g (3 oz) fresh white
   breadcrumbs

finely grated zest of 1 lemon
2 tablespoons chopped fresh parsley
salt and freshly ground black pepper
about 25g (1 oz) Parmesan, grated
a little paprika for dusting

TO SERVE
a little salad of baby spinach leaves,
   lightly dressed

1 If the mussels need cooking, wash in plenty of cold water, scraping away any barnacles and pulling off the beards. Discard any mussels that are open and which do not close when tapped sharply. Put the mussels and water or wine into a large pan, cover and cook over a high heat for 3–4 minutes, shaking the pan occasionally, until the mussels have just opened. (Discard any that remain closed.) Drain the mussels, then break off and discard the empty half shells. Put the mussels still in the outer shell in a single layer on a baking tray.

2 Melt the butter in a small pan, add the onion and garlic and cook gently until soft but not coloured.

3 Skin the tomatoes, cut in half, remove the seeds and chop the flesh finely.

4 Mix the breadcrumbs with the onion and garlic, tomato, lemon zest, parsley and season with salt and pepper.

5 Top each mussel with about a teaspoon of stuffing, sprinkle with Parmesan and dust with paprika.

6 Grill under a hot preheated grill for about 3–5 minutes, or until they are crisp and golden brown. Serve immediately on a bed of dressed fresh baby spinach.

cook now, eat later

TO PREPARE AND COOK AHEAD Prepare to the end of step 5 up to 6 hours ahead. Cover and keep in the fridge until needed. Grill to serve until piping hot right through.

TO FREEZE Not suitable.

TO COOK IN THE AGA Use the Boiling Plate for steps 1 and 2. Arrange the stuffed mussels on a baking sheet and slide on to the second set of runners in the Roasting Oven for about 10 minutes or until golden brown and crisp.

Char-grilled vegetables with goat's cheese ᵛ

This starter looks stunning, and all the preparation can be done the day before. I like the peppers peeled but it is not essential. If you don't like goat's cheese, the vegetables are delicious topped with Parma ham and shavings of Parmesan cheese.

Serves 6

1 aubergine, halved lengthwise	1 fat garlic clove, cut in half
2 small courgettes	salt and freshly ground black pepper
2 red peppers, cut in half, seeds removed	2 × 100g (4 oz) Capricorn goat's cheeses
olive oil	(a roll shape, with skin on)
1 tablespoon balsamic vinegar	4 tablespoons fresh white breadcrumbs
a pinch of fresh thyme leaves	paprika

1 Thinly slice the aubergine and courgettes on the diagonal.

2 Put the peppers skin side up under a hot grill, about 10cm (4 in) away from the heat, and grill until the skins scorch and blacken. Put the hot peppers in a plastic bag, seal the top and allow to sweat. When the peppers are cool enough to handle, peel the skin off and slice the flesh neatly.

3 Mix the aubergine, courgette and 1 tablespoon of oil together in a large plastic bag or bowl. Heat a ridged grill pan or frying pan. When the pan is very hot, char-grill the aubergine and courgettes in batches until tender (turn only once). Transfer to a bowl, add the sliced red pepper, 2 tablespoons of oil, the vinegar, thyme and garlic. Season well.

4 Remove the ends from the cheeses leaving the skin around the sides, and cut each cheese into 3 even discs. Brush the cheese with a little olive oil and roll the cheese in seasoned breadcrumbs, to give a fine coating. Place on a piece of non-stick paper on a baking sheet.

Preheat the oven to 200°C/400°F/Gas 6.

5 About 15 minutes before serving, put the vegetables in a serving dish, cover tightly with foil and put into the preheated oven to warm through. About 5 minutes prior to assembling, increase the oven temperature to 220°C/425°F/Gas 7. Sprinkle the cheese with paprika and slide on to the top shelf of the oven for about 5–7 minutes until just beginning to melt around the edges but still firm in the middle (these do melt quite a lot, this is part of the charm!).

6 Remove the garlic from the vegetables and spoon the vegetables on to 6 individual plates. With a fish slice, lift a slice of warmed goat's cheese on to each pile of vegetables. Drizzle the dressing from the vegetables around the plate. Serve with warm ciabatta bread.

recipe continued overleaf

TO PREPARE AND COOK AHEAD Prepare the char-grilled vegetables, continuing to the end of step 3, and marinate them overnight in the fridge. The coated cheese may also be left on non-stick paper or foil in the fridge overnight, covered in clingfilm.

TO FREEZE Not suitable.

TO COOK IN THE AGA Scorch the red peppers on non-stick paper on a baking tray at the very top of the Roasting Oven for about 20 minutes, or until black, then follow the rest of step 2. To finish and assemble, bake the vegetables in the Simmering Oven, 15 minutes before serving. Heat the cheese in the Roasting Oven for 3–5 minutes until just beginning to melt.

TIP To get attractive ridges on meat, fish or vegetables, etc. when char-grilling, you need a ridged grill pan (most of them are non-stick). First butter or oil the food being char-grilled and season with salt and pepper. Heat the pan until very hot, then add the food to the pan until cooked.

Individual baked artichoke and Parma ham galettes

This artichoke recipe is Ann Usher's, an inspirational cook who now lives in France, and she gives it to her many guests from England. I have added a puff pastry case, but one with no bottom, which makes it wonderfully light. Dead easy, the pastry case is cut from ready-rolled puff pastry.

Serves 6–8

1 × 285g jar Sacla seasoned artichoke hearts in oil	1 × 375g packet ready-rolled puff pastry
	a little milk
50–75g (2–3 oz) sliced dry-cured ham (Parma, Black Forest, Serrano or Bayonne)	paprika
1 × 250g tub creamy full-fat fromage frais	TO SERVE
4 drops Tabasco sauce	1 small packet rocket leaves
100g (4 oz) Gruyère cheese, grated	olive oil
salt and freshly ground black pepper	balsamic vinegar

Well grease a large baking tray or line a baking tray with non-stick paper. Preheat the oven to 220°C/425°F/Gas 7.

1 Drain the artichoke hearts in a colander then on kitchen paper to mop up all the oil. Cut the artichokes so that you have 24 pieces, 3 pieces to put into each pastry case.

2 Remove surplus fat from the ham and cut the ham into small pieces. Mix these with the fromage frais, Tabasco and two-thirds of the Gruyère. Season to taste with salt and pepper.

3 Unroll the pastry on to a lightly floured surface and cut 8 squares, about 7.5–10cm (3–4 in). Stamp a 5cm (2 in) circle out from the centre of each pastry square. Lift each square of pastry on to the prepared baking tray. Brush the pastry with milk.

4 Put 3 pieces of artichoke in the centre circles of the pastry squares, and top with the fromage frais mixture, piling it up slightly. Sprinkle the reserved grated cheese over the artichokes and the pastry then dust with paprika.

5 Bake in the preheated oven for about 15–20 minutes or until the pastry is risen and golden brown.

6 Serve at once with rocket salad, dressed with a little olive oil and balsamic vinegar.

cook now, eat later

TO PREPARE AHEAD Drain and cut the artichokes, and cover. Mix together the ham, fromage frais, Tabasco, Gruyère and seasoning, and cover. Cut the squares of pastry, stamp out the circles, put on the prepared baking trays, and cover tightly. Store everything overnight in the fridge. Assemble up to 6 hours ahead.

TO FREEZE Not suitable.

TO COOK IN THE AGA Bake on the floor of the Roasting Oven for about 7–10 minutes until the pastry is risen and golden brown.

Prawn and avocado tians

A very impressive first course, far more exciting than avocado filled with prawns! These are made in metal rings bought from Lakeland Limited or good cook shops. You could use ramekin dishes lined with clingfilm (or see the tip on page 149).

Instead of prawns, for a change use the same weight of flaked cooked salmon or crab. Make sure that you use horseradish cream for this recipe (also sometimes called creamy horseradish), and not a hot horseradish sauce, or the flavour will completely overpower the prawns. Even so, it is wise to taste the horseradish cream and cut down the amount used in the recipe if you think it necessary.

Serves 6

4 medium tomatoes

3 small avocados, firm but just ripe

juice of about ½ lemon

1 tablespoon salad dressing

salt and freshly ground black pepper

2 spring onions, very finely shredded

175g (6 oz) shelled cooked tiger prawns

2 generous tablespoons 'light' low-calorie
   mayonnaise

2 good teaspoons creamed
   horseradish

TO SERVE

lightly dressed green salad leaves,
   including rocket or lamb's lettuce

chopped fresh parsley

You will need six 7cm (2¾ in)
   metal rings.

1 First, dip the tomatoes in boiling water to loosen the skins. Plunge straightaway into cold water and remove the skins. Quarter each tomato, remove the seeds, then slice the flesh into thin strips and drain on kitchen paper.

2 Cut the avocados in half, remove the stone and peel. Cut each half to fit the base of the metal rings: avocado halves vary slightly, but I usually find that just cutting off the pointed end is about right. Mix with the lemon juice to prevent discolouring. (Mix the trimmings of avocado with the lemon juice too, then use them up in a green salad later.)

3 Place a piece of clingfilm on a flat tray just large enough to stand your rings on top. Put the large piece of avocado in the base of each ring. Press down firmly using a small ramekin or perhaps a straight-sided glass that fits inside the ring. Add the tomato and salad dressing to the empty bowl, then season with salt and pepper and add the spring onions. Spoon on top of the avocado. Press down again (some liquid will come out of the bottom of the ring when you press down).

recipe continued overleaf

4 In the same now empty bowl, mix the prawns, mayonnaise, horseradish and some salt and pepper. Spoon the prawns on top of the tomato (they will come slightly over the top of the ring).

5 Cover the tray and rings with clingfilm and chill for at least 4 hours.

6 Arrange some dressed green salad leaves on 6 plates. Using a fish slice or broad palette knife lift a ring into the centre of each plate. Carefully lift off the ring. Sprinkle the prawns with parsley. Serve with warm rolls.

cook now, eat later

TO PREPARE AHEAD The tians can be made the day before, kept in the fridge and turned out on the day, a couple of hours in advance of serving. Keep in the fridge, though.

TO FREEZE Not suitable.

Crab cakes with mild chilli sauce

Fresh and frozen crabmeat can be difficult to come by, so I use tinned. I found John West was the best. The dipping sauce I use is Blue Dragon sweet chilli dipping sauce. I would always make these cakes ahead, and reheat them so that there is no last-minute frying. Serve 1 crab cake each as a first course or 2 each as a main course.

Makes 12 cakes

450g (1 lb) fresh white crabmeat,
    or 3 x 170g cans John West white
    crabmeat, drained
2 tablespoons chopped fresh parsley
40g (1½ oz) cream crackers, finely crushed
    in a polythene bag with a rolling pin
1 egg
2 tablespoons 'light' low-calorie
    mayonnaise

1–2 teaspoons Dijon mustard
2 tablespoons lemon juice
1 tablespoon sweet chilli dipping sauce
salt and freshly ground black pepper
a little sunflower oil for frying

MILD CHILLI SAUCE
8 tablespoons sweet chilli dipping sauce
4 tablespoons crème fraîche

1 Measure the crabmeat into a bowl and mix with the parsley and cream crackers.

2 Break the egg into a small bowl and whisk in the mayonnaise, mustard, lemon juice and chilli sauce and season with salt and pepper. Fold most of this mixture into the crabmeat but try not to break up the lumps of meat too much (you may not need all the egg mixture, mix only until it binds together). Taste and add more seasoning if necessary.

3 Shape the mixture into 12 patties, put them on a plate, cover with clingfilm and chill for at least 1 hour.

4 Heat the sunflower oil in a large frying pan and cook the crab cakes for 2–3 minutes until hot all the way through, crisp and richly golden, turning once. (These can be served straightaway.)

5 Mix the sweet chilli sauce and crème fraîche and keep in the fridge until needed. Serve a spoonful of the sauce on the side of the plate with the crab cakes.

cook now, eat later

TO PREPARE AND COOK AHEAD Fry the crab cakes the day before, then reheat them, uncovered, in the oven preheated to 200°C/400°F/Gas 6 for about 10 minutes or until hot through.

TO FREEZE The crab cakes do not freeze particularly well.

TO COOK IN THE AGA Fry the crab cakes ahead on the Boiling Plate, then reheat them, uncovered, on non-stick paper on the second set of runners in the Roasting Oven for about 7–10 minutes until hot right through.

Asparagus and quail's egg salad

This attractive plate of salad is light and tempting. You could swap some of the ingredients: salmon for prawns, and perhaps add some dressed artichoke hearts.

Serves 6

12 quail's eggs	1 heaped teaspoon finely chopped
18 asparagus spears or, if large, 9 cut in	fresh chives
half lengthways (cut off the very	1 heaped teaspoon finely chopped
woody ends)	fresh parsley
2 tablespoons 'light' low-calorie	salt and freshly ground black pepper
mayonnaise	6 slices smoked salmon
2 tablespoons half-fat crème fraîche	1 lemon, cut into 6 wedges

1 Bring the quail's eggs to the boil in cold water and boil for a further 3 minutes. Drain, run under cold water and peel.

2 Cut the asparagus into tips of 5cm (2 in) in length, and the remaining stalks into chunks of just under 1 cm (½ in), peeling first with a potato peeler if the stems are a bit woody. Cook the stems in boiling water for 4–5 minutes, adding the tips during the final 2 minutes. Drain and refresh thoroughly in very cold water.

3 Measure the mayonnaise, crème fraîche and herbs into a bowl with the well-dried asparagus stalks. Season well with salt and pepper.

4 Arrange a slice of smoked salmon around the edge of each starter plate, spoon the mayonnaise and asparagus mixture into the centre of each plate, and top with 4 halved quail's eggs and 3 asparagus tips. Serve with a lemon wedge and brown bread.

cook now, eat later

TO PREPARE AND COOK AHEAD If you have room in your fridge, assemble completely on individual plates, cover tightly and keep in the fridge for up to 12 hours. Or complete steps 1–3, cover and keep in the fridge for up to 6 hours.

TO FREEZE Not suitable.

TIP Quail's eggs are easier to peel if not too fresh, but well within their sell-by date. I boil them for 3 minutes, then plunge them into cold water and peel from the pointed end straightaway. When offering with drinks, pile in a bowl but leave a few with their shells on as this looks more attractive. Serve with celery salt.

Twice-baked tomato and feta soufflés ^V

Everyone loves a hot first course, so one that can be made ahead and reheated at the last minute is a real winner. This also makes a delicious lunch dish, served with crusty bread and a mixed leaf salad. Who said making a soufflé was difficult!

Sun-blushed tomatoes are now available in larger supermarkets. They are half-dried tomatoes which are less chewy than the usual sun-dried tomatoes and can be used in their place.

The recipe makes enough to fill 7 ramekins.

Serves 6

40g (1½ oz) butter, plus extra for greasing	3 eggs, separated
40g (1½ oz) plain flour	25g (1 oz) Parmesan, freshly grated
300ml (½ pint) milk	500ml (18 fl oz) tomato passata,
salt and freshly ground black pepper	seasoned with a few drops of
100g (4 oz) feta cheese, cut into cubes	Worcestershire sauce
50g (2 oz) sun-blushed tomatoes,	1–2 tablespoons chopped fresh chives
chopped	

Generously butter and base-line 6 or 7 ramekins. Preheat the oven to 220°C/425°F/Gas 7.

1 Melt the butter in a generously sized saucepan, remove from the heat and blend in the flour. Return to the heat, and cook the roux for 30 seconds, stirring all the time. Add the milk bit by bit and bring to the boil, stirring constantly. Simmer until the sauce is thick and smooth.

2 Remove the pan from the heat and beat in some seasoning, the feta and drained sun-dried tomatoes. When these are well incorporated, stir in the egg yolks.

3 Whisk the egg whites until stiff, and stir 1 tablespoon into the sauce to loosen the mixture. Carefully fold in the remaining egg white. Spoon into the prepared ramekins, place them in a small roasting tin, and pour boiling water into the tin to come half-way up the ramekins.

4 Cook in the bain-marie in the preheated oven for 10 minutes, then turn them around and cook for a further 8–10 minutes until golden and springy to the touch. Leave to stand for 5 minutes in the ramekin dishes to shrink back.

5 Butter a shallow gratin dish (large enough to hold the little soufflés so that they just do not touch) and sprinkle over half of the Parmesan. Pour the seasoned passata into the gratin dish. Run the blade of a small palette knife around the edges of the soufflés, unmould them carefully, and put them into the gratin dish. Sprinkle the remaining Parmesan over the surface.

6 Return to the oven for about 10–15 minutes until golden and bubbling. Scatter over the chives to garnish.

cook now, eat later

TO PREPARE AND COOK AHEAD Up to 48 hours ahead, turn the cooked soufflés out on to the buttered and Parmesan-sprinkled dish. Don't sprinkle with the remaining Parmesan or pour in the passata yet. Cover with foil and keep in the fridge. Continue as from step 5.

TO FREEZE Freeze the wrapped, cooked soufflés for up to 1 month. Thaw at room temperature for about 6 hours. Reheat as from step 5.

TO COOK IN THE AGA Bake the soufflés in the bain-marie on the grid shelf on the floor of the Roasting Oven for 15–20 minutes. After 10 minutes, when the soufflés are a perfect golden brown, turn round if necessary and slide the cold shelf on the second set of runners and continue cooking until they are springy to the touch. Leave for 5 minutes in the dishes to shrink back. Continue with steps 5 and 6, baking in the Roasting Oven, but without the cold shelf, for another 15–20 minutes or until the soufflés are puffed up and golden.

TIP Passata is sieved tomatoes, and is wonderful to use in soups, stews, pasta dishes or sauces. It can be bought in cartons or bottles. If only using half the bottle, freeze the remainder, but use within 2 months. Like tomato purée, it goes off quickly in the fridge.

FISH

Our fish shops have sadly nearly diminished, but the good news is that our supermarkets are beginning to excel in fish – offering a wide selection and, thankfully, increasingly knowledgeable staff. I have chosen fish that we can get hold of easily now, such as salmon, sea bass, tuna and swordfish, but I haven't covered fish such as Dover sole, skate, halibut, turbot, herring or mackerel. These I think are best cooked very simply by grilling or pan-frying, and you don't need a recipe for that.

Fish must always be extremely fresh, and the major clue to freshness is its smell. It must not smell *too* fishy. You should ideally buy fish on the day you are going to start preparing it, and this ought to be either the day of cooking or the day before. The other major factor when dealing with fish is that it must not be overcooked. Fish is translucent at first, and is cooked when it becomes opaque. Marginally *under*cook if you are going to keep fish warm (as is usual when feeding guests), as the fish will continue to cook slightly. And although I know it's fashionable in restaurants now to serve fish raw, or virtually so, I don't think this is a good idea at home.

Fish is notorious for cooking quickly, for needing to be done at the last minute, for not 'lasting' very well when being kept hot, and for not freezing (apart from my fish cakes, of course). But even fish, if you have bought the best quality, can be prepared in advance to a certain extent. A number of the recipes here require marination, and then the fish is cooked at the last moment. Other recipes suggest searing one side of the fish in advance, which starts the fish off, and then you only need to cook the fish for a few minutes before serving. The other huge advantage of this advance searing is that you can get rid of any fishy smells well before your guests arrive. A lot of people are put off cooking fish because they feel that it all has to be done at the last minute, getting themselves, the kitchen and even the rest of the house, smelling of fish. This need not be so if you think – and cook – ahead.

Double Haddock and Herb Fish Cakes

Baked Sole Florentine

Baked Cod with Pesto and Parmesan Mash

Fresh Swordfish Steaks on a Bed of Lentils

Salmon Tranche with Fresh Lime and Ginger Sauce

Teriyaki Tuna

Char-grilled Sea Bass on a Bed of Vegetables

Moroccan Fish

For more fish ideas, see:

Smoked Haddock Bouillabaisse (see page 14)

Fresh Salmon and Dill Terrines (see page 20)

Garlic-stuffed Grilled Mussels (see page 22)

Prawn and Avocado Tians (see page 29)

Crab Cakes with a Mild Chilli Sauce (see page 30)

Chilli-hot Monkfish Pasta with Crisp Green Vegetables (see page 132)

Salmon Coulibiac (see page 136)

Reggiori Pasta Bake with Tuna and Two Cheeses (see page 186)

Salmon and Fennel Fish Pie (see page 190)

Double haddock and herb fish cakes

I'm suggesting that these fish cakes are oven baked, but if preferred they may be fried in butter and oil until crisp and brown. They freeze well before cooking and can be eaten for any meal!

Serves 6–8

450g (1 lb) main-crop potatoes, peeled

salt and freshly ground black pepper

225g (8 oz) smoked undyed haddock fillet

225g (8 oz) fresh haddock fillet

a good 25g (1 oz) butter

3 heaped tablespoons chopped
  fresh parsley

1 heaped tablespoon chopped fresh dill

2 good tablespoons 'light' low-calorie
  mayonnaise

a few drops of Tabasco sauce to taste

fresh white breadcrumbs

LIGHTER HERB SAUCE

4 tablespoons chopped fresh parsley

2 tablespoons chopped fresh dill

4 tablespoons low-fat crème fraîche

4 tablespoons 'light' low-calorie
  mayonnaise

4 spring onions, finely shredded

1 tablespoon chopped capers

juice of ½ lemon

salt and freshly ground black pepper

a little caster sugar

Preheat the oven to 200°C/400°F/Gas 6.

1 Cut the potatoes into even-sized pieces and cook in boiling salted water until tender. Drain well.

2 Season the fish with salt and pepper and cut the fillets in half if large. Wrap the fish in a foil parcel with the butter. Bake in the preheated oven for about 12–15 minutes until the fish is opaque and flakes easily.

3 Mash the potatoes with the buttery juices from the cooked fish. Skin the fish, discarding any bones, and flake into a bowl with the mashed potatoes. Add the herbs, mayonnaise and Tabasco and season well with salt and pepper.

4 Divide into 12 even-sized round fish cakes. Roll the fish cakes in the breadcrumbs. Cover and chill if time allows.

5 For the sauce, mix all of the ingredients together. Season, adding a dash of sugar.

6 Preheat a heavy baking sheet in the oven with the temperature increased to 220°C/425°F/Gas 7. Lightly grease the baking sheet with butter and arrange the fish cakes on it in a single layer. Brush with melted butter and bake for about 20–25 minutes until crisp, golden and hot through. Serve with the herb sauce and lemon or lime wedges.

recipe continued overleaf

TO PREPARE AND COOK AHEAD Prepare the fish cakes to the end of step 4. Cover and store in the fridge for up to 1 day. Make the sauce on the day.

TO FREEZE Open-freeze the prepared fish cakes at the end of step 4 until solid, then transfer to a freezer bag and freeze for up to 4 months. To thaw, remove the fish cakes from the freezer bag and put in a single layer on a baking tray. Cover and thaw for 3 hours at room temperature or overnight in the fridge.

TO COOK IN THE AGA To cook the fish, put the fish parcel in a roasting tin and bake on the lowest set of runners in the Roasting Oven for about 10–12 minutes or until the fish is opaque and flakes in the centre when tested with a fork.

To cook the fish cakes, preheat a baking sheet or large roasting tin on the floor of the Roasting Oven for 5 minutes, and brush generously with butter. Bake the fish cakes on the sheet or tin for 4 minutes on the floor of the Roasting Oven, turn over and bake for a further 4 minutes until golden brown and piping hot. If need be, they can be kept warm for up to 40 minutes, covered, in the Simmering Oven.

TIP Keep fresh herbs in the fridge, so useful to have to hand for garnishing, or to chop into pasta or salad at the last minute. Put in a jug with a little water with a plastic bag over the top to keep fresh. Basil, a herb that is used to a warm climate, is best kept *out* of the fridge.

Baked sole florentine

A wonderfully easy fish recipe which takes very little time to cook. Lemon sole fillets are quite expensive, but you can keep the cost down by choosing small fish. Ask the fishmonger to skin and fillet 6 fish for you. When assembling the dish, try to match up the fillets in size.

Serves 6

25g (1 oz) butter, plus extra for greasing	200ml (7 fl oz) double cream
salt and freshly ground black pepper	2–3 heaped tablespoons freshly grated
1 medium onion, finely chopped	Parmesan
225g (8 oz) fresh young spinach, washed	paprika
and finely shredded	coarsely chopped fresh parsley
a little freshly grated nutmeg	lemon wedges to serve
12 lemon sole fillets, skinned	

Butter and season a shallow ovenproof dish large enough to take the fish. Preheat the oven to 200°C/400°F/Gas 6.

1 Melt the butter in a large frying pan, add the onion and cook over a low heat for 10–15 minutes until soft. Add the spinach to the pan and cook over a high heat for a few minutes until the spinach has wilted and all of the water has been driven off. Season with salt, pepper and nutmeg. Remove from the heat and allow to become completely cold.

2 Press the spinach mixture with a kitchen towel to remove any excess moisture.

3 Season the fish with salt and pepper on both sides and arrange the 6 largest fillets skinned side down in the prepared oven dish. Divide the spinach mixture in the middle of each fillet in the dish. Using a small sharp knife cut a slit about 5cm (2 in) long in the centre of each of the remaining 6 fillets. Position the top fillet in a mirror image over the spinach and bottom fillet, allowing the filling to just show through.

4 Season the cream with salt and pepper and pour all over the fillets. Sprinkle with the Parmesan and dust with paprika. Bake in the preheated oven for about 25–30 minutes until the fish flesh is white and firm and cooked through. The baking time may alter according to the depth of dish used.

5 Garnish with parsley and serve with lemon wedges.

cook now, eat later

TO PREPARE AND COOK AHEAD Prepare to the end of step 3. Cover and keep in the fridge for up to 1 day.

TO FREEZE Not suitable.

TO COOK IN THE AGA Bake at the top of the Roasting Oven for about 10–15 minutes until the fish flesh is white and firm and cooked through. The baking time may alter according to the depth of dish used.

Baked cod with pesto and Parmesan mash

An all-in-one dish that can be prepared ahead. This could also be made with salmon fillet. Serve with a green salad or petits pois.

Serves 6

about 500g (1 lb 2 oz) main-crop potatoes, peeled	6 large tomatoes, skinned, seeded and cut into long strips
a good knob of butter	a few sprigs of fresh basil, chopped
a little milk	75g (3 oz) Parmesan, coarsely grated
6 teaspoons pesto	a little paprika
salt and freshly ground black pepper	parsley to garnish
6 × 175g (6 oz) tail fillets of cod, skinned	

Lightly grease a large baking tray. Preheat the oven to 220°C/425°F/Gas 7.

1 Bring the potatoes to the boil in salted water, cover and simmer for about 15–20 minutes or until tender. Drain well, then mash, adding butter, a little milk, the pesto and some seasoning.

2 Season the cod fillets on both sides then place on the greased baking tray. Spread one-sixth of the mashed potato on each fillet. Mix the strips of tomato and basil together, season, and arrange over the mash. Sprinkle with Parmesan and dust with paprika.

3 Bake in the preheated oven for about 15 minutes or until the fish has turned white. Serve immediately, garnished with parsley.

cook now, eat later

TO PREPARE AND COOK AHEAD If the fish is very fresh and the mashed potato cold, you may cover the assembled uncooked fish and store in the fridge for up to 1 day.

TO FREEZE Not suitable.

TO COOK IN THE AGA Bake on the top set of runners of the Roasting Oven for about 10–15 minutes until the fish has turned white.

Fresh swordfish steaks on a bed of lentils

Swordfish steaks are without bone and are delicious, but take great care not to overcook otherwise they will be tough. They are sometimes two-tone in colour – pinky-grey along where the bone was – but don't worry, this is normal.

If you have a ridged grill pan it makes all the difference to the look of the recipe – the steaks are attractive with the char-grilled stripes.

Serves 6

250g (9 oz) dried Puy lentils	4–5 tomatoes, skinned, seeded and cut
1.1 litre (2 pints) stock, or water and	into neat strips
stock cube	3 tablespoons coarsely chopped fresh
salt and freshly ground black pepper	parsley
2 teaspoons fresh thyme leaves	6 × 150–175g (5–6 oz) swordfish steaks
2 tablespoons olive oil, plus extra for	
greasing	
1 large onion, chopped	TO SERVE (OPTIONAL)
200g (7 oz) oyster mushrooms, thickly	a little olive oil and balsamic vinegar
sliced	mixed together
	chopped fresh parsley

1 Rinse the lentils, drain, and bring to the boil in a pan with the stock or water and stock cube, with a little salt and pepper and the thyme. Simmer uncovered for about 15–20 minutes until just soft. Drain and set aside.

2 Heat the oil in a large frying pan, add the onion after a few minutes, cover and soften over a low heat for about 15 minutes. When soft, add the mushrooms and fry over a high heat for about 2 minutes. Season well with salt and pepper. Add the lentils, tomatoes and parsley to the pan and check the seasoning.

3 Heat a ridged grill pan or large frying pan over a high heat until very hot. Lightly oil and season the fish steaks on both sides. Brown the steaks for about 2 minutes on each side.

4 Spoon the hot lentil mixture into a hot serving dish (or on to individual plates), and serve the swordfish steaks on top. Spoon about a teaspoon of balsamic vinegar and olive oil over the top of each steak, garnish with parsley and serve.

cook now, eat later

TO PREPARE AND COOK AHEAD The lentil mixture can be made up to 12 hours ahead.
Fry the steaks in a hot ridged grill pan for about 45–60 seconds on one side only
until golden brown – this can also be done about 12 hours ahead – then cool and
keep in the fridge. To serve, arrange the lentils in a serving dish large enough to
hold the 6 steaks, cover with foil and reheat in the preheated oven at
200°C/400°F/Gas 6 for about 15–20 minutes. Remove the foil, transfer the steaks to
the top of the lentils (browned side up) and cook for a further 10–15 minutes
(depending on the thickness of the steaks) until cooked in the centre but not dry.

TO FREEZE Not suitable.

TO COOK IN THE AGA Cook the lentils on the Simmering Plate until tender. Cook
the onion in the Simmering Oven, covered, for about 15 minutes until tender.
Finish step 2 on the Simmering Plate. Put the lentil mixture into a serving dish. Fry
the steaks in a hot ridged grill pan on one side only for about 45 seconds on the
Boiling Plate. Reheat the serving dish, filled with the lentils and covered with foil,
on the grid shelf on the floor of the Roasting Oven for about 10–15 minutes.
Arrange the steaks, browned side up, on the lentils, and return to the same position
in the Roasting Oven for a further 10–15 minutes until just cooked.

Salmon tranche with fresh lime and ginger sauce

Char-grilling or frying fish is a smelly, smoky business, and to do this earlier in the day – or even the day before – is a huge advantage. Then all you have to do is blast the fish in the oven for a few minutes, and make a quick sauce.

Serves 6

6 × 150g (5 oz) slices of salmon fillet (cut from the centre of the salmon), skinned
finely grated zest and juice of 2 limes
1 × 5cm (1 in) piece fresh ginger root, grated

6 tablespoons dark soy sauce
freshly ground black pepper
225g (8 oz) butter
3 tablespoons chopped fresh chives

1 Check that the salmon is without any small bones. (The easiest way to remove any is with tweezers.)

2 Put the zest and juice of the limes, ginger and soy sauce into a bowl. Season the salmon with pepper and turn in the marinade in the bowl. Cover with clingfilm, and leave to marinate in the fridge for a few hours or overnight.

3 Lift the fish out of the marinade, pat the top dry with kitchen paper and spread with a little of the butter. Strain the marinade into a small jug.

4 Preheat a ridged grill pan over a high heat on the hob for a few moments. When very hot add the salmon, butter side down, and char-grill until golden, about 1 minute. Lower the heat and continue to cook the salmon until it is just cooked through, 6–10 minutes, depending on the thickness of the fish. Lift out and keep warm.

5 Next quickly make the sauce and glaze. Pour the marinade into a pan, bring to the boil then whisk in knobs of the remaining butter until it has all been included. Stir with a wooden spoon over a high heat for a few moments until shining. No need to season. Take care not to reduce too much.

6 Arrange a fish fillet on each plate. Add the chives to the sauce and add a spoonful of sauce over one end of the fish. Serve with a green vegetable.

recipe continued overleaf

cook now, eat later

TO PREPARE AND COOK AHEAD Marinate the salmon for a few hours or overnight. At step 4 brown the salmon quickly on one side, lift out, cool quickly, cover and keep in the fridge until ready to cook. You can do this the night before. To serve, arrange the fillets in an ovenproof serving dish, grilled side up, and reheat in the preheated oven at 200°C/400°F/Gas 6 for about 6–10 minutes. To test when done, check to see the fish is cooked through (or almost, if keeping it warm). Quickly make the sauce using the marinade, butter and chives before serving.

TO FREEZE Not suitable.

TO COOK IN THE AGA Brown the salmon in a hot frying pan or ridged grill pan for 1 minute on one side on the Boiling Plate. Transfer to a roasting tin, grilled side up. Bake the salmon on the grid shelf on the floor of the Roasting Oven for about 8 minutes or until the fish is a matt pale pink all through.

Teriyaki tuna

It is worthwhile buying a good-quality marinade. If overcooked, tuna can be dry, but this marinade helps to keep it moist.

Serves 6

6 × 175g (6 oz) fresh tuna steaks, about
   2.5cm (1 in) thick

100ml (4 fl oz) teriyaki marinade
   (buy in a bottle)

1 × 2.5cm (1 in) piece fresh root ginger,
   grated

1 tablespoon clear honey

6 spring onions, finely sliced

2 tablespoons sunflower oil

1 red pepper, seeded and finely sliced

1 Put the tuna steaks into a shallow, non-metallic dish. Mix together the teriyaki marinade, ginger, honey and spring onions and pour over the tuna steaks. Cover and leave to marinate in the fridge for a few hours, turning once.

2 Heat the oil in a large non-stick frying pan. When very hot, add the tuna steaks and cook for about 2–3 minutes on each side, depending on the thickness. Lift out and keep warm.

3 Add the red pepper to the pan and stir-fry quickly. Pour in the marinade with about 200ml (7 fl oz) water, and bring to the boil. Boil until of a thin syrupy consistency.

4 Lift the slices of red pepper from the sauce with a slotted spoon and spoon on top of the tuna steaks to garnish. Offer the remaining sauce separately. Serve with boiled rice and a green salad.

cook now, eat later

TO PREPARE AHEAD Marinate the tuna ahead. Keep in the fridge overnight or until needed.

TO FREEZE Not suitable.

TO COOK IN THE AGA Cook the tuna in a preheated pan on the Boiling Plate, followed by the ingredients for the sauce.

Char-grilled sea bass on a bed of vegetables

Supper in one dish. Prepare the vegetables and fish ahead, leaving only a salad to make on the day.

Serves 6

butter	4 large tomatoes, skinned, quartered
700g (1½ lb) new potatoes	and seeded
I large onion, cut into wedges	4 red peppers, cut in half and seeded
olive oil	50g (2 oz) black olives in oil, drained
I garlic clove, crushed	6 sea bass fillets, with the skin left on
salt and freshly ground black pepper	chopped fresh parsley and basil

Lightly butter a 25 × 38cm (10 × 15 in) ovenproof dish. Preheat the oven to 200°C/400°F/Gas 6, and preheat the grill.

1 Boil the potatoes and onion in salted water until the potatoes are only just done. Drain and cut the potatoes into even pieces about 2.5cm (1 in) square, or a bit smaller. Return to the pan with the onion, 1–2 tablespoons of the oil, the garlic, salt and pepper.

2 Arrange the potatoes and onion down the centre of a large ovenproof dish, scatter the tomatoes on top, and season with salt and pepper.

3 Put the peppers cut side down on to the grill rack and grill under the hot grill until the skin blisters and blackens. Whilst still hot put the peppers into a polythene bag and seal the top so that they sweat. When cool enough to handle, peel off the skin and cut the flesh into quarters.

4 Mix the peppers with the olives, season and coat with olive oil. Spoon the peppers and olives down either side of the potatoes. Cover with foil.

5 Slash the fish skin and brush with a little oil. Season the fish and fry skin side down in a very hot frying pan or ridged grill pan over high heat for about 1 minute until the skin is crisp and brown. The flesh will still be raw underneath.

6 Reheat the vegetables, covered, in the preheated oven for about 20 minutes, until very steamy and exceedingly hot. Remove the foil.

7 Put the fish on top of the potatoes, skin side up, and bake for about 8–10 minutes until just cooked. Sprinkle with parsley and basil to serve.

recipe continued overleaf

TO PREPARE AND COOK AHEAD Prepare the vegetables ahead to the end of step 4. Keep in a cool place until needed (overnight if you like). Sear the skin of the fish for 1 minute, as in step 5. Remove to a plate and chill until ready to cook (again, this could be done the night before). Keep them separate. Reheat and cook as in steps 6 and 7.

TO FREEZE Not suitable.

TO COOK IN THE AGA Char-grill the fish ahead, skin side down in a ridged grill pan, on the Boiling Plate for about 1 minute until the skin is crisp and brown. About 25 minutes before serving, reheat the vegetables on the floor of the Roasting Oven for about 20 minutes. Put the fish on top of the potatoes, skin side up, and roast at the top of the Roasting Oven for 8 minutes.

Moroccan fish

Use monkfish if you prefer. Harissa paste is a hot chilli paste used in North African dishes.

Serves 6–8

2 tablespoons olive oil	1kg (2¼ lb) skinned cod, cut into
350g (12 oz) small courgettes,	large pieces
roughly cubed	1 x 400g can chickpeas, drained
450g (1 lb) red onions, roughly chopped	50g (2 oz) black olives, stoned
3 level teaspoons harissa paste	salt and freshly ground black pepper
1 x 400g can chopped tomatoes	2 tablespoons each of chopped fresh
500ml (18 fl oz) tomato passata	coriander and parsley

1 First make the sauce. Heat the olive oil in a large frying pan (one with a lid) or shallow casserole dish, add the courgettes and fry over a high heat for 10 minutes until golden. Lift out with a slotted spoon and transfer to a bowl.

2 Add the onions to the pan and fry for 10 minutes until beginning to colour. Stir 2 teaspoons of harissa paste into the onions and cook for a further 2–3 minutes.

3 Return the courgettes to the pan, then mix in the chopped tomatoes and tomato passata. Bring to the boil, cover then simmer gently for about 30 minutes.

4 Marinate the fish with the remaining harissa paste, as the sauce is cooking.

Preheat the oven to 200°C/400°F/Gas 6.

5 Add the marinated fish to the casserole with the chickpeas and olives. Push the fish down into the sauce, season with salt and pepper, cover and cook in the preheated oven for 15–20 minutes. The fish should be white rather than opaque.

6 When cooked, gently stir the coriander and parsley into the sauce and serve with rice or couscous.

cook now, eat later

TO PREPARE AND COOK AHEAD Cook the sauce to the end of step 3 but only for 20 minutes. Cool, cover and keep in the fridge for up to 24 hours. Marinate the fish a few hours ahead, cover and keep in the fridge. Reheat the sauce very gently over a low heat, then continue with step 5.

TO FREEZE Cool the sauce at the end of step 3, pack and freeze for up to 3 months. Thaw overnight at cool room temperature, bring back to the boil and bubble for 3–4 minutes then use to complete the recipe. Do not freeze the fish and sauce together.

TO COOK IN THE AGA At step 2, cook the onions covered in the Simmering Oven for about 10–15 minutes. At step 5, bring to the boil, cover and transfer to the Simmering Oven for about 15–20 minutes.

POULTRY AND GAME

I have given you some interesting chicken recipes here, which are very 'international' in flavour, plus a trio of duck and pheasant ideas. In all of them I have removed the skin, which makes them cook in a slightly different way. It also means that the final dish will contain much less fat, which many people prefer nowadays. (Keep the bones and skin from poultry and game and use them for stock, and if you like duck 'crackling', simply cut the skin into strips and fry or bake until crisp.)

Overcooking is always a fear with prime poultry and game cuts such as chicken and pheasant breasts. Although *under*cooking in advance is not generally considered to be sensible, provided you have bought best-quality meat, and cool and chill it properly, this should not be a problem, and will be safe. Several of the recipes here can be marinated or partially prepared in advance before being finished at the last moment. But most can be completely cooked at least the day before, then reheated until piping hot to serve. And of course a majority of them can be cooked well ahead and frozen. All you have to do then is defrost, reheat well, garnish and serve.

A primary consideration when cooking casserole-type dishes to be reheated from cold or frozen is the quantity of sauce. Some of the sauce can be lost through evaporation during reheating, and so we have taken this into account. Most people like a *lot* of sauce! And always taste any dish in the kitchen before reheating after chilling or freezing: it's too late to add significant seasoning by the time you taste it at the table.

Glazed Oriental Duck with Pak Choi

Pan-fried Pheasant with a Mango Sauce

Braemar Pheasant

Chardonnay Chicken with Artichoke Hearts

Thai Fragrant Chicken

Chicken Olives Provençal

Chilean Chicken

Italian Chicken with Olives and Tomato

Lemon and Thyme Chicken with Winter-roasted Vegetables

For more poultry and game ideas, see:

Spicy Turkey Fajitas (see page 140)

Turkey Salad with Avocado, Bacon and Pesto Dressing (see page 141)

Piquant Chicken with Basil (see page 142)

Chilled Gazpacho Chicken (see page 195)

Cockatrice (see page 196)

Traditional Roast Turkey (see page 224)

Glazed oriental duck with pak choi

Duck breasts with a wonderful flavoured sauce, which may be made well ahead. If you buy breasts other than Barbary — which will probably be smaller — adjust the cooking times accordingly. Buy pineapple juice in a carton, the kind that you would buy for breakfast.

Serves 6

6 duck breasts, skin removed	SAUCE
salt and freshly ground black pepper	1½ level tablespoons cornflour
a little soft butter	100g (4 oz) dark muscovado sugar
1 tablespoon sunflower oil	450ml (¾ pint) pineapple juice
350g (12 oz) pak choi, sliced into 5cm	3 tablespoons white wine vinegar
(2 in) pieces (keep the stems and	1½ tablespoons soy sauce
leaves separate)	1½ tablespoons hoisin sauce
	1 tablespoon sunflower oil
	a good 4cm (1½ in) fresh root ginger,
	grated
	2–3 garlic cloves, crushed

1 Season the duck breasts with salt and pepper and spread with a little soft butter on one side. Heat a ridged grill pan, and sear the duck breasts, butter side down at first, for 1 minute on each side. Lower the heat and cook the duck for about a further 7 minutes if you like the duck pink in the centre, or 10 minutes if you like it well done. Rest the duck for 10 minutes before slicing.

2 To make the sauce, measure the cornflour, sugar and 6 tablespoons of the pineapple juice into a bowl and mix until smooth. Add the remainder of the pineapple juice, the vinegar, soy and hoisin sauces.

3 Heat 1 tablespoon of the oil in a frying pan and gently cook the ginger and garlic for a few moments. Pour in the contents of the bowl, and stir continually as the mixture comes to the boil. Strain the sauce, check the seasoning, and add any duck juices.

4 Heat 1 tablespoon of the oil in a large frying pan, add the pak choi stems, and stir-fry over a high heat for 2–3 minutes until almost tender. Toss in the leaves and stir-fry until just wilted. Season.

5 To serve, spoon the pak choi into the centre of 6 hot plates. Arrange the duck slices on the pak choi and spoon the hot sauce around the outside.

recipe continued overleaf

cook now, eat later

TO PREPARE AND COOK AHEAD Sear the duck up to 24 hours ahead. Cool, cover and chill in the fridge. Continue with step 1 to cook the duck, allowing more cooking time as the duck will be being heated from cold. The sauce can also be made a couple of days ahead.

TO FREEZE Not suitable.

TO COOK IN THE AGA Sear the duck breasts on a ridged grill pan on the Boiling Plate for 1 minute on each side. Lift on to a roasting rack in the roasting tin and slide on to the grid shelf on the floor of the Roasting Oven for 7 minutes if you like the duck pink in the centre, or 10 minutes if you like it well done. Rest the duck for 10 minutes before slicing. Make the sauce on the Simmering Plate.

Pan-fried pheasant with a mango sauce

A quick way to cook pheasant breasts without allowing the pheasant to become dry.

Serves 6

olive oil	3 tablespoons Worcestershire sauce
1 large onion, finely chopped	450ml (¾ pint) double cream
6 pheasant breasts, skin removed	paprika
3 tablespoons mango chutney	chopped fresh parsley

Preheat the oven to 200°C/400°F/ Gas 6.

1 Heat 1 tablespoon of olive oil in a large sauté pan, fry the onion, lower the temperature, cover and cook gently until tender, about 10–15 minutes. Spread over the base of a shallow ovenproof dish.

2 Pan-fry the pheasant breasts in a little more oil on a high heat on both sides until brown. Slice each breast into 3 slices on the diagonal, then put on top of the soft onion and season with salt and pepper. They should still be pink in the middle.

3 Stir the mango chutney and Worcestershire sauce into the cream, season and pour over the pheasant. Dust with paprika, and cook in the preheated oven for about 15–20 minutes until the pheasant is tender and the sauce is brown.

4 Allow to rest for a few minutes, before scattering with parsley. Serve with mashed potatoes to mop up the sauce, and perhaps fresh broccoli.

cook now, eat later

TO PREPARE AND COOK AHEAD Cook the onion and pan-fry the pheasant 1 day ahead until barely cooked. Cool, cover and keep separately in the fridge until ready to complete. Mix together the ingredients for the sauce, cover and keep in the fridge until needed. To serve, slice each breast into 3, put into the ovenproof dish, and pour over the sauce. Reheat for about 20 minutes at the same temperature as above until piping hot and bubbling.

TO FREEZE Complete to the end of step 3. Cool quickly, pack and freeze for up to 2 months. Thaw thoroughly and reheat as above until piping hot.

TO COOK IN THE AGA Cook the onion in the Simmering Oven for about 20 minutes or until tender. Pan-fry the pheasant breasts on the Boiling Plate then continue with steps 2 and 3 towards the top of the Roasting Oven for about 10–15 minutes.

Braemar pheasant

This recipe uses pheasant breasts. Use the legs for a casserole or stock. Leeks and bacon go really well in game recipes.

Serves 6

100g (4 oz) thickly sliced bacon, cut into strips	1 tablespoon cranberry or redcurrant jelly
2 leeks, coarsely shredded	a few sprigs of fresh parsley
2 tablespoons sunflower oil	1 large sprig of fresh thyme
6 pheasant breasts, skin removed	1 bay leaf
25g (1 oz) plain flour	salt and freshly ground black pepper
300ml (½ pint) apple juice	a generous amount of chopped fresh parsley
300ml (½ pint) chicken stock	

1 Heat a non-stick frying pan and add the bacon. Cook gently, stirring occasionally, for a few minutes, then add the leeks and cook until the leeks are beginning to brown and the bacon is crisp. Remove the leeks and bacon to a plate.

2 Heat the oil in the same pan and fry the pheasant breasts quickly on a high heat until browned all over. Lift out and add to the bacon and leeks. Add the flour to the pan and cook, stirring, for 1 minute. Gradually blend in the apple juice, stock and cranberry or redcurrant jelly. Bring to the boil, stirring until thickened.

3 Return the browned pheasant, bacon and leeks to the pan, and add the parsley sprigs, thyme, bay and seasoning. Bring to the boil, cover and simmer gently for about 10–15 minutes until the pheasant is tender. Keep warm and rest for 15 minutes before serving.

4 Taste the sauce for seasoning, remove the parsley sprigs, thyme and bay leaf, and sprinkle over lots of chopped parsley to serve. Good with mashed potato.

cook now, eat later

TO PREPARE AND COOK AHEAD Prepare to the end of step 3. Cool quickly, cover and keep in the fridge for up to 1 day. Reheat until piping hot to serve.

TO FREEZE It will freeze but take care not to overcook the pheasant in the first place. Freeze and thaw completely. Reheat until piping hot, stirring.

TO COOK IN THE AGA Cook steps 1 and 2 on the Boiling Plate. At step 3, bring to the boil on the Boiling Plate, cover and transfer to the Simmering Oven for about 10–15 minutes until the pheasant is tender.

Chardonnay chicken with artichoke hearts

This special chicken casserole goes really well with creamy mashed potato or basmati and wild rice. There is plenty of sauce with this recipe so if you want to give 2 thighs each, or serve more people, add up to 6 more thighs. If you like a slightly less rich version, leave out the crème fraîche.

Serves 6–8

8 chicken thighs on the bone, skin removed	25g (1 oz) plain flour
salt and freshly ground black pepper	300ml (½ pint) Chardonnay or dry white wine
1 tablespoon olive oil	225g (8 oz) small chestnut mushrooms, whole
15g (½ oz) butter	
2 large onions, roughly chopped	1 × 400g can artichoke hearts
2 garlic cloves, crushed	2 tablespoons full-fat crème fraîche
1 teaspoon caster sugar	4 tablespoons chopped fresh parsley

1 Season the chicken thighs with salt and pepper. Heat the oil and butter in a large deep frying pan and brown the chicken thighs all over. Lift out on to a plate.

2 Add the onions, garlic and sugar to the oil remaining in the pan and cook over a low heat for about 15–20 minutes until tender.

3 Turn up the heat and allow the onions to brown. Sprinkle in the flour, thoroughly blending, add the wine and stir well. Bring to the boil, stirring until thickened.

4 Return the chicken to the pan with the mushrooms, season and bring to the boil. Simmer over a low heat, or transfer to a slow oven at 160°C/325°F/Gas 3 and cook until the chicken is tender, about 45 minutes.

5 Drain the artichokes, cut in half and add to the chicken. Heat through gently then add the crème fraîche, check the seasoning and stir in most of the parsley.

6 Sprinkle with the remaining parsley and serve with basmati and wild rice or mashed potato.

cook now, eat later

TO PREPARE AND COOK AHEAD Prepare to the end of step 4. Cool quickly, cover and keep in the fridge for up to 24 hours. Reheat until piping hot, stirring in the artichokes towards the end of reheating. Stir in the crème fraîche and parsley to serve.

TO FREEZE Cool quickly and freeze at the end of step 4 for up to 3 months. Thaw overnight in the fridge and reheat until piping hot. Continue with steps 5 and 6.

TO COOK IN THE AGA Complete step 1 on the Boiling Plate. Cook the onion at step 2, covered, in the Simmering Oven for 20 minutes. Return to the Boiling Plate for steps 3 and 4. Add the chicken and mushrooms, bring to the boil and cover. Transfer to the Simmering Oven and cook until tender, about 45 minutes. Continue with steps 5 and 6.

Thai fragrant chicken

There is a wonderful light and subtle flavour to this chicken dish. Ideally, it should be made the day before so that the flavours infuse, and then can be reheated gently to serve. We like a generous amount of sauce but if you like less, reduce the amount of stock. It would then also make a thicker sauce, which you may prefer.

Serves 6

5 large chicken breasts, skin and bone removed, cut into thin strips	1 × 2.5cm (1 in) piece cinnamon stick
salt and freshly ground black pepper	seeds of 6 cardamom pods, crushed
2 tablespoons sunflower oil	2 teaspoons ground cumin
1 large onion, finely chopped	1 bay leaf
2 garlic cloves, crushed	150ml (¼ pint) chicken stock
1 × 3cm (1–1½ in) piece fresh root ginger, grated	1 × 200ml carton coconut cream (UHT)
½ teaspoon garam masala	finely grated zest and juice of ½–1 lime
	chopped fresh coriander

1 Season the chicken with salt and pepper. Heat half the oil in a large non-stick pan, add the chicken and quickly brown. Lift out on to a plate. It is best to do this in batches.

2 Heat the remaining oil in the frying pan, then add the onion, garlic and ginger. Cook for a few minutes over a high heat, then cover and cook gently over a low heat for about 10 minutes until soft.

3 Add the garam masala, cinnamon, cardamom, cumin and bay leaf, and stir for 1 minute. Add the browned chicken. Blend in the stock and the coconut cream, stirring continually until it comes to the boil. Season, cover with the lid and simmer gently for about 5 minutes, or until the chicken is cooked. Remove and discard the cinnamon stick and bay leaf. Stir in the lime zest and juice.

4 Sprinkle with coriander, and serve with *Aromatic Thai Rice* (see page 143).

recipe continued overleaf

TO PREPARE AND COOK AHEAD Make to the end of step 3 the day before. Cool quickly then store in the fridge. Reheat gently until piping hot, then scatter with coriander.

TO FREEZE Not suitable.

TO COOK IN THE AGA Sear the chicken on the Boiling Plate. Cook the onion, garlic and ginger for a few minutes on the Boiling Plate, then cover and transfer to the Simmering Oven for about 20 minutes until soft. Return to the Boiling Plate to add the spices, chicken, stock and coconut cream, return to the boil, cover and transfer to the Simmering Oven for about 10 minutes until cooked.

Chicken olives Provençal

This is a super family supper dish. Boneless chicken thighs are readily available from all good supermarkets. The stuffing and sauce are very easy to do and the chicken doesn't need browning ahead.

Serves 4–6

3 large good-quality pork sausages	SAUCE
25g (1 oz) black olives, stoned and finely chopped	2 tablespoons dark soy sauce
finely grated zest of 1 lemon	1 scant tablespoon Worcestershire sauce
1 tablespoon finely chopped fresh thyme	1 tablespoon runny honey
1 tablespoon finely chopped fresh sage	2 teaspoons grainy mustard
salt and freshly ground black pepper	1 × 400g can chopped tomatoes
8 chicken thighs, skin and bone removed	
25g (1 oz) Parmesan, coarsely grated	
chopped fresh parsley to garnish	

You will need an ovenproof dish about 28 × 23cm (11 × 9 in). Preheat the oven to 190°C/375°F/Gas 5.

❙ Slit each sausage skin lengthways and remove the meat. Put the sausagemeat into a bowl, add the olives, lemon zest, thyme, sage, salt and pepper, and mix well.

2 Unfold and lay out the chicken thighs (smooth side down). Season with salt and pepper and fill with a tablespoon of the sausagemeat stuffing (where the bone would have been). Bring each edge of the chicken towards the middle, over the stuffing. Arrange in the dish, join side down. Season the thighs all over.

3 Blend together the sauce ingredients in a bowl and pour over the thighs, ensuring all are covered. Sprinkle Parmesan over the chicken.

4 Cook in the preheated oven for about 30–40 minutes until the chicken is tender and the sauce is piping hot.

5 Garnish with parsley and serve with herby mashed potatoes.

cook now, eat later

TO PREPARE AND COOK AHEAD Complete to the end of step 3, cover and keep in the fridge for up to 8 hours. Cook as directed in step 4, ensuring that the chicken is cooked and the sauce is piping hot before serving. Or complete to the end of step 4, cool quickly, cover and keep in the fridge for up to 24 hours. Reheat at 200°C/400°F/Gas 6 for about 20–25 minutes, or until the chicken and sauce are piping hot.

TO FREEZE The raw stuffed chicken thighs freeze very successfully. Defrost thoroughly in the fridge overnight before cooking, as from step 4. Or freeze the cooked completed dish. Thaw for 6 hours at room temperature or overnight in the fridge. To reheat, follow the above.

TO COOK IN THE AGA For step 4, slide the dish on to the second set of runners in the Roasting Oven for about 25–30 minutes, or until the chicken is tender and the sauce boiling.

Chilean chicken

A quick and easy dish that looks good enough to serve for a dinner party. There is no sauce to make at the last minute, as the savoury butter can be poured over.

Serves 6

6 chicken breasts, skin and bone removed	SAVOURY BUTTER
	115g (4½ oz) butter
salt and freshly ground black pepper	2–3 hot red chillies, seeded
a few fresh coriander leaves to garnish	3 sun-dried tomatoes in oil, drained
	1 large garlic clove, peeled
	a small bunch of fresh coriander

Preheat the oven to 220°C/425°F/Gas 7.

1 Place all the savoury butter ingredients, plus some salt and pepper, in a food processor and blend until well mixed and almost smooth. Chill if time allows.

2 Beat out the chicken breasts between 2 sheets of clingfilm until thin, using a rolling pin.

3 Reserve a small amount of the savoury butter. Season the chicken breasts with salt and pepper and spread the butter over them. Roll up tightly (like a beef olive) lengthways.

4 Take 6 pieces of foil, big enough to enclose one chicken breast in each. Rub any reserved butter over the foil and put a chicken breast on to each piece. Season again, then fold the foil around the chicken and seal at the side by crimping together.

5 Put the chicken parcels on to a baking tray and cook in the preheated oven for about 20 minutes, depending on the size of the chicken breasts, until cooked. Allow to rest for a further 10 minutes.

6 Lift out of the foil, slice the chicken breasts on the diagonal, and spoon over the buttery juices. Garnish with coriander and serve with rice.

recipe continued overleaf

cook now, eat later

TO PREPARE AND COOK AHEAD Make the butter up to a week ahead, and keep in the fridge. Fill and roll the chicken as in step 3, wrap individually in foil as in step 4 and store in the fridge up to 24 hours ahead. Cook and serve as in steps 5 and 6.

TO FREEZE Wrap and freeze the filled, rolled and uncooked chicken for up to 2 months. (NB the chicken must be fresh.) Thaw overnight in the fridge. Continue with steps 5 and 6.

TO COOK IN THE AGA Put the foil parcels directly on the Boiling Plate (with the foil join to one side) for 1½–2 minutes to brown the chicken. Turn the whole parcel over into the small roasting tin and transfer to the floor of the Roasting Oven for 12–15 minutes, depending on the size of the chicken breasts. Allow to rest for a further 10 minutes.

TIP It's wonderful to keep a variety of flavoured butters in the fridge to use on jacket potatoes, for bread (as you would garlic bread), and to stir into pasta. The butter here is wonderful and brightly coloured too.

Italian chicken with olives and tomato

An especially easy supper dish made from store-cupboard ingredients. It reheats well too!

Serves 6

12 chicken thighs, skin removed, bone in	300ml (½ pint) chicken stock, or water
salt and freshly ground black pepper	and stock cube
1–2 tablespoons olive oil	2 tablespoons white wine vinegar
2 large onions, roughly chopped	100g (4 oz) about 12 pitted prunes,
2 fat garlic cloves, crushed	halved
1 level tablespoon caster sugar	1 × 190g jar olive and tomato sauce
2 level tablespoons plain flour	(such as Sacla Olive and Tomato)
	a lot of chopped fresh parsley

1 Season the chicken thighs with salt and pepper.

2 Heat the oil in a frying pan and fry the onions and garlic for a few minutes. Cover with a lid and cook gently for about 20 minutes until the onions are tender.

3 Add the sugar to the onions and return to a high heat for a few minutes to lightly brown and caramelise the onions and to drive off any excess liquid. Sprinkle in the flour and mix well. Draw to one side and add the stock, stirring. Return to the heat and bring to the boil. Allow to thicken, adding the vinegar, prunes, and some salt and pepper.

4 Add the chicken to the pan and bring back to the boil. Cover the pan and cook over a gentle heat for about 20–30 minutes (turning the chicken once), until the chicken is tender. Cut into a thigh with a sharp knife to ensure the juices run clear. If still bloody continue to cook over a gentle heat until the juices do run clear.

5 Stir in the whole jar of olive and tomato sauce, and heat until piping hot. Check the seasoning. If the sauce is a bit thick, add a little more stock or water.

6 Scatter with parsley and serve with basmati and wild rice or tagliatelle and a green salad.

cook now, eat later

TO PREPARE AND COOK AHEAD Cook completely ahead to the end of step 5, 24 hours ahead. Cool quickly, cover and refrigerate. Reheat carefully, gently stirring, in a pan on the hob until piping hot. Or reheat in the oven preheated to 200°C/400°F/Gas 6 for about 30 minutes, stirring occasionally. Add a little stock or water if the sauce is thick.

TO FREEZE Freezes well. Cool the cooked chicken quickly and freeze in a freezer container for up to 3 months. Thaw for about 6 hours at room temperature or overnight in the fridge.

TO COOK IN THE AGA Cook the onions, covered, in the Simmering Oven for about 20 minutes until tender. Use the Boiling Plate for step 3. For step 4, transfer the covered pan to the Roasting Oven for about 10 minutes, and then to the Simmering Oven for a further 10 minutes, or until the chicken is cooked.

Lemon and thyme chicken with winter-roasted vegetables

A one-pot whole meal. It is essential to cook the vegetables in a wide shallow casserole dish or roasting tin: if the dish is too deep, the vegetables will not take on the crisp, brown-roasted finish. For a heartier dish, use leg or breast joints and cook for about 25 minutes on top of the vegetables.

Serves 6

6 chicken breasts, skin removed	3 large old potatoes, peeled and cut into
juice of 2 lemons	chunks (roast potato size)
a good bunch of fresh thyme	225g (8 oz) peeled parsnips, cut in half
2 tablespoons olive oil	lengthways
300ml (½ pint) chicken stock	225g (8 oz) medium carrots, peeled and
1 tablespoon cornflour	cut in half lengthways
	3 tablespoons olive oil
VEGETABLES	salt and freshly ground black pepper
350g (12 oz) peeled swede, cubed	a few sprigs of fresh thyme
275g (10 oz) peeled sweet potato, cut	2 medium courgettes, cut into thick slices
into chunks (roast potato size)	

1 Marinate the chicken breasts in the lemon juice, thyme leaves and 1 tablespoon of the olive oil for a few hours, or overnight if time allows.

Preheat the oven to 200°C/400°F/Gas 6.

2 Toss all the vegetables, except the courgettes, in the oil in a large shallow casserole dish or roasting tin, and season with salt and pepper. Add the thyme sprigs. Cook in the preheated oven for about 1½–2 hours, turning occasionally, until the vegetables are cooked and tinged with colour, stirring from time to time. (Do not cover.)

3 Lift the chicken breasts from the marinade (reserve the marinade). Heat the remaining oil in a frying pan and brown the chicken breasts on both sides.

4 About 15 minutes before the vegetables are finished, toss the courgettes in with the vegetables and put the chicken breasts on top of the vegetables in the oven. Return the dish to the oven and cook for a further 15 minutes or so or until the chicken is tender. Remove the thyme sprigs to serve.

5 Pour the reserved marinade into the frying pan (in which the chicken breasts were browned) and add the chicken stock. Bring to the boil. Slake the cornflour with a little water and add to the pan. Bring to the boil and taste for seasoning. Serve this sauce with the chicken and vegetables.

cook now, eat later

TO PREPARE AND COOK AHEAD Marinate the chicken up to 24 hours ahead. Prepare and slightly undercook the vegetables. The night before, brown the chicken as in step 3, cool, cover and keep in the fridge. Continue with steps 4 and 5, cooking for about 20 minutes.

TO FREEZE Not suitable.

TO COOK IN THE AGA Cook the vegetables in a roasting tin on the floor of the Roasting Oven for just under 1 hour, stirring half-way through. Brown the breasts on the Boiling Plate. Toss in the courgettes, put the browned chicken breasts on top of the vegetables, and return to the second set of runners in the Roasting Oven for a further 15 minutes or until the vegetables and chicken are tender.

MEAT

Meat stews and casseroles can, like poultry dishes, be completely cooked ahead and chilled for a day or so, or frozen. They should be cooked until tender, but never overcooked, or the meat chunks could fall apart when reheated. Again as with chicken, tasting is vital, especially when cooking ahead. Taste, then adjust the seasoning as appropriate, but not just with salt and pepper. If something has a lot of tomatoes in it, you may need a pinch of sugar. Perhaps some lemon juice or redcurrant jelly may be needed. You as the host are the first to start when your friends come for a meal, and how sad it would be if your first mouthful alerted you to the fact that you should have added some balsamic vinegar, more pepper or a dash of lemon, or enriched it with some cream.

It's not a fallacy that some meat and poultry dishes just do taste better when reheated. The flavours, especially of spicy dishes and those containing red wine, have time to mature and come together. And even with dishes that cannot be fully prepared ahead, some flavour advantages can be gained: a stuffing can flavour raw meat during an overnight chilling, and a marinade can add flavour and tenderise it at the same time.

I have included some roasts here which of course cannot be cooked ahead – but elements of the individual dishes can (Yorkshire pudding and roast potatoes, for instance), and this will help you have more time when you need it. Even just ordering the meat well in advance from your butcher, particularly of a less common cut such as saddle of lamb, will save you time in a sense. And you can store prime cuts in the fridge for a few days, which will allow them to mature and gain even more flavour. (Remove the butcher's plastic, and rewrap in greaseproof paper, or non-stick parchment paper.)

Marinated Roast Lamb with Minted Couscous and Whisky Gravy

Roast Saddle of Lamb with Rosemary and Redcurrant Gravy

Mexican Spicy Lamb

Tagine of Lamb

Pork Escalopes with Apple and Onion

Roast Pork Fillets with Apple and Fennel Sauce

Roast Prime Rib of Beef with Beetroot and Horseradish

Pan-fried Fillet Steaks with Fresh Herb Sauce

Venison and Beef with Port and Apricots

Calf's Liver with Caramelised Onions and Balsamic Gravy

For more meat ideas, see:

Thai Pork Curry (see page 144)

Baked Sausages with Double Onion Marmalade (see page 145)

Glazed Apple Gammon (see page 189)

The Perfect Whole Roast Fillet of Beef with Thyme (see page 198)

Steak and Mushroom Pie with Dauphinoise Potato Topping (see page 200)

Lancashire Lamb Shanks (see page 202)

Marinated roast lamb with minted couscous and whisky gravy

The minted couscous is roasted with the lamb. You may need to cover it with foil to stop it getting too brown, or if preferred roast it in a separate buttered dish. Use a meat thermometer to obtain the perfect roast.

Serves 6

1.5kg (3¼ lb) leg of lamb (before boning), main leg bone removed to the ball and socket
1 tablespoon cornflour
350ml (12 fl oz) water
chopped parsley to garnish

MARINADE
7 tablespoons soy sauce
50g (2 oz) light muscovado sugar
4 tablespoons whisky
juice of ½ lemon
1 tablespoon Worcestershire sauce

ROASTED COUSCOUS
350g (12 oz) couscous
600ml (1 pint) stock, or stock cube and water
275g (10 oz) ready-to-eat dried apricots, snipped into pieces
4 generous tablespoons bottled mint sauce
4 fat garlic cloves, crushed
salt and freshly ground black pepper

Preheat the oven to 220°C/425°F/Gas 7. Butter an oblong, ovenproof dish, about 28 × 33 × 5cm (11 × 13 × 2 in), large enough to hold the couscous and lamb.

1 Measure the marinade ingredients into a strong polythene bag, add the lamb to the bag and seal the top. Put in the fridge overnight. Drain off the marinade liquid the next day and reserve.

2 Measure the couscous into a bowl, pour on the boiling stock, add the other ingredients and season well with salt and pepper. Spoon all the couscous into the buttered dish, leaving space for the lamb. (At this stage the couscous is slightly sloppy: as it cooks, it firms up.)

3 Transfer the lamb to the dish, placing it upside down. Insert a meat thermometer and roast in the preheated oven for about 30 minutes. Turn the lamb over after this time, and stir the couscous, covering the couscous with foil if it is getting too brown. Reduce the oven temperature to 200°C/400°F/Gas 6 and cook for a further 1–1½ hours until the temperature on the thermometer reads about 75°C for medium lamb. Remove from the oven and rest, covered, for 15 minutes whilst making the gravy.

4 For the gravy, mix the cornflour, marinade and water together in a small pan and whisk over a high heat until thickened. Adjust the seasoning. Carve the meat and put alongside the couscous in the dish. Scatter with parsley to serve.

cook now, eat later

TO PREPARE AHEAD Marinate the lamb overnight in the fridge. The couscous can be prepared as in the beginning of step 2, and the bowl put in the fridge overnight. Transfer the couscous to the buttered dish and cook as from step 3.

TO FREEZE Not suitable.

TO COOK IN THE AGA At step 3, slide the dish on to the second set of runners in the Roasting Oven for about 1 hour. You may need to cover the couscous with foil. Allow to rest, covered, for 15 minutes in the Simmering Oven.

TIP Meat thermometers are wonderful. I use the one on a spike with a spinning dial (I trust it more than a digital one!). You can add it at the beginning or at the end of cooking but ensure it's inserted into the thickest part of the meat, not touching any bone. To be sure the thermometer is working, put the spike into boiling water and check the temperature.

Roast saddle of lamb with rosemary and redcurrant gravy

A saddle of lamb is both loins cut between the best end of neck and the leg. It also includes the kidneys and tail which are tied and skewered to the joint in a decorative fashion, ready for roasting.

Ask your butcher to bone the joint (for easy carving) but then to tie it back on the bone in its original position so that the joint will retain maximum flavour. For carving, simply untie the string. It is a good idea to order the saddle well ahead. The raw meat will also be improved if left maturing in the fridge for up to 2 days – it will have a better flavour.

The resting time after roasting is very important as well (see recipe).

Serves 12–14

3kg (6½ lb) saddle of lamb, skinned, boned, excess fat removed and reassembled (see above)	GRAVY
	2 tablespoons sunflower oil
salt and freshly ground black pepper	a knob of butter
butter for greasing	1 large onion, roughly chopped
2 tablespoons redcurrant jelly	1 sprig of fresh rosemary
1–2 garlic cloves, cut into slivers	1 heaped tablespoon plain flour
1 large sprig of fresh rosemary, plus extra for garnish	450ml (¾ pint) stock
	150ml (¼ pint) red wine
	1 tablespoon redcurrant jelly
	1 teaspoon lemon juice
	1 teaspoon Worcestershire sauce
	a little gravy browning (optional)

Preheat the oven to 200°C/400°F/Gas 6.

1 First make the gravy base which can be made well ahead. Heat the oil and butter in a wide-based pan, add the onion and rosemary, and fry for a few minutes. Stir in the flour, and cook for a few minutes. Pour on the stock and wine, stirring continually until smooth, and bring to the boil. Season with salt, pepper, redcurrant jelly, lemon juice and Worcestershire sauce. Just before carving tip the pan juices into the gravy and strain out the onion and rosemary. Add a little gravy browning to colour if necessary.

2 Line a large roasting tin with foil, season the lamb all over and sit the meat in the roasting tin. Cover the kidneys with buttered foil (this way they won't overcook). Spread the redcurrant jelly over the saddle. Tuck some of the garlic and rosemary under the lamb and the remainder around the sides of the meat.

3 Roast in the preheated oven for 12 minutes per 450g (1 lb) for medium lamb. Check after 20 minutes to see how the saddle is browning. When a perfect rich brown, cover loosely with foil. Turn the tin around half-way through the cooking time. Allow the lamb to rest for 45 minutes and up to 1 hour, still leaving it in the roasting tin covered with foil in an oven at 140°C/275°F/Gas 1. (If you have no oven space take it from the very hot oven and at once cover and wrap the tin with a thick towel.)

4 To serve, cut in half lengthways down the back, then thickly slice each loin on the diagonal. This I find best, though the more old-fashioned way of carving is to carve strips parallel to the back bone down the full length of the meat.

5 Garnish with rosemary. Serve with the gravy, mint sauce and redcurrant jelly.

Smaller short saddle

Serves 6–8

1 short saddle, weighing 1.75kg (3½ lb)

Roast for 15 minutes per 450g (1 lb). Rest for 45 minutes to 1 hour before carving.

cook now, eat later

TO PREPARE AHEAD Order the meat from the butcher well ahead. Keep in the fridge for up to 2 days prior to roasting. Make the gravy base the day before.

TO FREEZE Not suitable.

TO COOK IN THE AGA Roast in the Roasting Oven with the roasting tin on the lowest set of runners, for slightly shorter times than the conventional oven, i.e. 10 minutes per 450g (1 lb).

Mexican spicy lamb

A warming casserole. Serve with tomato and basil salad and chunky garlic bread. Double up for a crowd, adding more cans of beans if they have very healthy appetites. If you have difficulty in getting black-eyed beans, use red kidney beans instead. For the young, use baked beans!

Serves 6–8

900g (2 lb) neck fillet of lamb	2 level tablespoons tomato purée
2 tablespoons sunflower oil	salt and freshly ground black pepper
2 garlic cloves, crushed	2 × 400g can black-eyed beans
1 large onion, sliced	2 generous tablespoons mango chutney
2 level tablespoons plain flour	
1 teaspoon ground cumin	TO SERVE
1 teaspoon ground coriander	sprigs of fresh coriander or mint
150ml (¼ pint) white wine	1 × 150g carton Greek yogurt
1 × 400g can chopped tomatoes	

Preheat the oven to 160°C/325°F/Gas 3.

1 Remove excess fat from the lamb and cut the flesh into large cubes. Heat half the oil in a large pan, add the lamb and brown in batches, keeping the heat high. Remove the lamb with a slotted spoon on to a plate.

2 Lower the heat and add the remaining oil and the garlic and onion to the pan. Allow to soften for a few minutes, then blend in the flour and spices and allow to cook for a further 2 minutes.

3 Add the wine, tomatoes and tomato purée to the pan along with the meat. Bring to the boil, season with salt and pepper, cover and transfer to the preheated oven for about 2 hours, until the meat is tender.

4 Drain and rinse the beans, add to the lamb with the mango chutney, and cook for about 10 minutes longer. Check the seasoning and tenderness.

5 Garnish with sprigs of coriander or mint. Serve with Greek yogurt seasoned and then mixed with 2 teaspoons chopped coriander or mint if liked.

recipe continued overleaf

cook now, eat later

TO PREPARE AND COOK AHEAD Prepare to the end of step 3. Cool quickly, cover and keep in the fridge for up to 2 days. Add the beans and mango chutney and reheat gently on the hob until piping hot.

TO FREEZE Cool quickly at the end of step 3, spoon into a freezer-proof container and freeze for up to 3 months. Thaw overnight in the fridge. Add the beans and mango chutney, and reheat until piping hot.

TO COOK IN THE AGA Sear the lamb on the Boiling Plate. Cook the onion on the Boiling Plate. At step 3, cook the lamb in the Simmering Oven for about 1½–2 hours or until the meat is tender.

Tagine of lamb

A traditional Moroccan dish, which is best made a day ahead and reheated.

Serves 6–8

1 tablespoon sunflower oil	1 teaspoon ground cinnamon
900g (2 lb) neck fillet of lamb or lean	1 tablespoon paprika
boneless leg or shoulder of lamb, cut	⅛ teaspoon hot chilli powder
into 2.5cm (1 in) pieces	a generous pinch of saffron stamens,
2 large onions, coarsely chopped	soaked in 3 tablespoons hot water
3 fat garlic cloves, crushed	2 tablespoons honey
175g (6 oz) ready-to-eat dried apricots,	1 × 800g can chopped tomatoes
quartered	salt and freshly ground black pepper
1 teaspoon ground ginger	chopped parsley to garnish

Preheat the oven to 160°C/325°F/Gas 3.

1 Heat the oil in a large frying pan and brown the lamb in batches. When brown remove with a slotted spoon and put on a plate to one side.

2 Add the onions and garlic to the pan, stir then cover and cook over a gentle heat for about 10–15 minutes until soft.

3 Increase the heat and add the apricots, spices, including the saffron and soaking liquid, honey, tomatoes and browned lamb to the pan. Bring to the boil, season, cover and cook in the preheated oven for about 2 hours until the meat is very tender. Check the seasoning.

4 Garnish with parsley and serve with couscous flavoured with mint and parsley.

cook now, eat later

TO PREPARE AND COOK AHEAD Complete to the end of step 3 a day ahead. Cool quickly, cover and keep in the fridge. Reheat on a low heat on the hob until piping hot.

TO FREEZE Cool quickly at the end of step 3. Pack into a freezer-proof container and freeze for up to 3 months. Thaw overnight in the fridge. Reheat until piping hot.

TO COOK IN THE AGA Sear the lamb on the Boiling Plate. Cook the onions in the Simmering Oven, covered, for 20 minutes. Cook the lamb to the end of step 3 in the Simmering Oven. Check from time to time, returning to the Boiling Plate if it is not cooking. Test if the meat is tender after about 2 hours, depending on the temperature of your Simmering Oven.

Pork escalopes with apple and onion

A very easy supper dish, but also good for a dinner party. I use wooden skewers and soak them first to prevent them burning.

Serves 6

6 × 225g (8 oz) lean pork chops	finely grated zest of 1 lemon
1 small onion, finely chopped	
1 large cooking apple, peeled, cored and	SAUCE
coarsely grated	150ml (¼ pint) apple juice
1 tablespoon chopped fresh parsley	1 teaspoon light muscovado sugar
1 tablespoon chopped fresh thyme	150ml (¼ pint) double cream

1 Remove the bone and some of the fat from the chops and slit horizontally through the meat from the bone side. Do not cut right through but leave an open pocket.

2 Heat a little butter in a frying pan and sauté the onion for a few minutes. Add the apple and gently soften for about 15 minutes. When the onion is tender, add the herbs, lemon zest and seasoning. Allow to cool.

3 Fill each chop with stuffing and secure with a wooden skewer. Season.

4 Heat a little oil in a large frying pan and fry the chops over a high heat for 3–4 minutes on each side. Turn the heat down and cook for a further 6–7 minutes. Transfer to a plate, cover while making the sauce, allowing the meat to rest. Keep warm.

5 Deglaze the pan with the apple juice and reduce over a high heat to about 3 tablespoons. Add the sugar and cream and boil for a couple of minutes. Season to taste. Sieve the sauce and serve with the pork chops.

cook now, eat later

TO PREPARE AND COOK AHEAD Brown the stuffed pork and slightly *under*cook 24 hours ahead. Reheat, covered, in the oven preheated to 200°C/400°F/Gas 6 for about 8 minutes to serve. The sauce can be made completely and sieved ahead.

TO FREEZE Not suitable.

TO COOK IN THE AGA Cook the onion and apple stuffing, covered, in the Simmering Oven for about 15–20 minutes, until tender. Brown the pork ahead on the Boiling Plate and reheat, covered, on the second set of runners in the Roasting Oven for about 6–8 minutes until hot. Reheat the sauce gently on the Simmering Plate.

Roast pork fillets with apple and fennel sauce

An all in one dish — inspired by one of our Aga ladies!

Serves 6

50g (2 oz) butter	STUFFING
2 × 225g (8 oz) fennel bulbs, trimmed and finely diced	175g (6 oz) onions, chopped
2 large cooking apples, peeled, cored and finely diced	150ml (¼ pint) water
salt and freshly ground black pepper	40g (1½ oz) butter
2 × 500g (1 lb 2 oz) pork fillets/tenderloins, trimmed	100g (4 oz) soft white breadcrumbs
fresh sage leaves to garnish	½ teaspoon dried sage

Preheat the oven to 220°C/425°F/Gas 7.

1 First prepare the stuffing. Put the onions and water together in a pan and bring to the boil. Cook for 10 minutes or until the onions are just tender but not soft. Drain and return the onions to the hot pan with the butter. Once the butter has melted, stir in the remaining stuffing ingredients, seasoning generously with salt and pepper. Allow to cool.

2 For the pork, melt the butter in a pan, add the fennel and apples and cook until almost soft. Season well with salt and pepper then spoon into the base of a medium roasting tin.

3 Cut the pork fillets about half-way through lengthways, and spread out into a broad 'V'. Spoon the stuffing into the 'V' and place on top of the bed of fennel and apple.

4 Cook in the preheated oven for 30–35 minutes until the pork is tender and the stuffing crispy and brown. Lift the pork out of the tin and keep warm.

5 Mash down the apple and fennel in the roasting tin to make a sauce. Slice the pork, garnish with sage leaves and serve with the apple and fennel sauce.

cook now, eat later

TO PREPARE AND COOK AHEAD Make the stuffing up to 24 hours ahead. Stuff the pork up to 24 hours ahead, cover and refrigerate until ready to cook.

TO FREEZE Not suitable.

TO COOK IN THE AGA Cook the stuffing on the Boiling Plate. Roast the stuffed fillets on the grid shelf on the floor of the Roasting Oven for 30 minutes or until tender.

Roast prime rib of beef
with beetroot and horseradish

Something very special. Prime rib (fore rib) and wing rib are first-class roasting cuts of meat.

Serves 8

1 × 2-rib joint, either prime rib cut short,
or wing rib cut short, 2.3kg (5 lb)
salt and freshly ground black pepper
1 large onion, unpeeled but thickly sliced

BEETROOT AND HORSERADISH
6 medium cooked beetroot, peeled
½ × 185g jar creamed horseradish

GOOD GRAVY
3 tablespoons dripping
1 very heaped tablespoon plain flour
75ml (⅛ pint) port
500ml (18 fl oz) beef stock
a dash of Worcestershire sauce
a little gravy browning

Preheat the oven to 220°C/425°F/Gas 7.

1 Sprinkle the beef fat with salt and pepper. Stand on end in a roasting tin just large enough for the joint on a bed of thick slices of unpeeled onion (the onion gives colour to the juices). If using a meat thermometer, insert into the meat in the thickest part going through to the centre of the meat. Transfer the meat to the centre of the preheated oven for 15 minutes, then lower the oven to 180°C/350°F/Gas 4. Roast as per chart (right) according to how well done you like your beef, basting from time to time.

2 Next prepare the beetroot. Cut the beetroot into short strips the thickness of a pencil, and mix with the horseradish. Season, transfer to an ovenproof dish, and cover with foil. Heat in the oven with the beef for the last 20 minutes until piping hot, stirring.

3 When the meat is done, check the thermometer and see chart (right). Lift out of the roasting tin, loosely cover with foil, and leave to rest in a warm place before carving. Discard the onion, having squeezed any juices into the tin.

4 Meanwhile, make the gravy. Skim off 3 good tablespoons of fat from the roasting tin. Pour the juices into a bowl and put in the fridge for the fat to rise to the top. Measure the flour into the tin, and whisk with the 3 reserved tablespoons of fat over the heat. Gradually add the port and stock, then the Worcestershire sauce. Remove the fat from the bowl of juices in the fridge, and add the juices to the gravy, along with a little gravy browning. Check the seasoning.

5 To carve, slip a sharp knife close to the bone to free the complete joint, then carve down across the grain. Serve with the beetroot and horseradish.

TO PREPARE AND COOK AHEAD Make the Yorkshire pudding and the beetroot and horseradish earlier in the day or the day before. Reheat in a preheated oven at 200°C/400°F/Gas 6: the beetroot and horseradish loosely covered in foil, stirring from time to time (about 20 minutes), and the Yorkshire pudding in the original roasting tin (about 10 minutes). You could par-roast the potatoes the day before as well.

ROAST POTATOES AND YORKSHIRE PUDDING It is extremely successful to roast potatoes or cook Yorkshire pudding a day ahead at home.

YORKSHIRE PUDDING For a rich Yorkshire pudding for 6, I use 100g (4 oz) plain flour, 3 eggs and 200ml (7 fl oz) milk, to fill a 20 × 30cm (8 × 12 in) roasting tin or 8 large individual ones in two 4-hole tins (small ones take about 15 minutes and large ones about 25 minutes). Heat the fat in the tin until really hot in the oven at 220°C/425°F/Gas 7 then pour in the batter. Cook until well risen, and leave in the tin. Keep in a cool place and reheat in a hot oven until hot and crisp, about 10–15 minutes.

ROAST POTATOES I parboil mine for 5 minutes then tip them into a colander to drain. Meanwhile, preheat the fat in the roasting tin or in a hot oven at 220°C/425°F/Gas 7 (Aga on the floor of the Roasting Oven) until very hot. Add the potatoes, turn in the fat, and return to the oven until pale golden and crisp, about 45 minutes, depending on size. Turn from time to time. Take out of the oven, remove any surplus fat/oil, and allow to cool in a larder or a safe place. Next day re-roast in the same temperature oven to re-crisp, about 20 minutes. Parsnips too can be done in the same way, but they need less roasting and reheating time – about 35 and 15 minutes respectively.

TO FREEZE Not suitable in general, but you could freeze the Yorkshire pudding.

TO COOK IN THE AGA Roast beef in the Roasting Oven with a meat thermometer and following the chart below. Cook the Yorkshire pudding in the small roasting tin on the lowest set of runners of the Roasting Oven. If making the Yorkshire Pudding ahead, reheat also in the Roasting Oven for about 8–10 minutes. Cook the potatoes on the floor of the Roasting Oven, and turn from time to time.

OVEN TEMPERATURES Individual ovens do vary, and these times are only a guide. A meat thermometer is the best way to ensure a properly cooked roast. I preheat the oven to 220°C/425°F/Gas 7 and roast for 15 minutes then follow the chart below.

Beef	Oven Temp	Time	Internal Temp
Rare	180°C/350°F/Gas 4	15 mins per 450g (1 lb)	60°C
Medium	180°C/350°F/Gas 4	20 mins per 450g (1 lb)	70°C
Well-Done	180°C/350°F/Gas 4	25 mins per 450g (1 lb)	75°C

Pan-fried fillet steaks with fresh herb sauce

It is difficult to make a small quantity of hollandaise sauce, unless you have a small herb processor. I have given instructions to make the hollandaise by hand – it really is quite easy!

Serves 6

6 x 175g (6 oz) thick fillet steaks	HOLLANDAISE/HERB SAUCE
salt and freshly ground black pepper	2 tablespoons lemon juice
a little butter	225g (8 oz) unsalted butter
1–2 tablespoons olive oil	4 egg yolks
	1 tablespoon each of chopped fresh
	parsley, marjoram and chives

1 To make the sauce, strain the lemon juice into a hot 2.2 litre (4 pint) heatproof mixing bowl. (Heat the bowl by pouring in water from the kettle just off the boil.) Melt the butter until bubbling in a small pan.

2 Add the egg yolks to the lemon juice and add some salt and pepper. Pour the hot butter slowly on to the egg yolks, in a steady stream, whisking continuously with a balloon whisk, or electric hand beater. The sauce should just hold its shape. Stir the herbs into the sauce and adjust the seasoning.

3 To cook the steaks, season them on both sides with salt and pepper. Spread one side of each with butter. Heat a large ridged grill pan or frying pan until very hot and add the oil. Add the steaks, buttered side down, and cook over a high heat for 2 minutes on each side for medium rare. Lower the heat and continue to cook until the steaks are to your liking (an extra 3 minutes on each side for well-done steaks).

4 Serve each steak with the fresh herb sauce, which melts over the hot steak.

cook now, eat later

TO PREPARE AND COOK AHEAD For steaks, complete step 3, cool at once, and put on a buttered baking sheet. When cold cover and keep in the fridge for up to 12 hours ahead. When ready to serve, reheat in a preheated oven at 220°C/425°F/Gas 7 for about 7–10 minutes until very hot. Make the fresh herb sauce on the day. Don't attempt to keep hot, leave at room temperature.

TO FREEZE Not suitable.

TO COOK IN THE AGA Fry the steaks on the Boiling Plate. Reheat the steaks on the second set of runners in the Roasting Oven for about 7 minutes.

Venison and beef with port and apricots

Casserole venison, ready cubed, can be found in many major supermarkets. Otherwise, use the meat from the shoulder or haunch.

Serves 6–8

about 3 tablespoons sunflower oil	1.1 litres (2 pints) beef stock
700g (1½ lb) stewing venison, cut into 2.5cm (1 in) pieces	300ml (½ pint) red wine
	2 tablespoons redcurrant jelly
700g (1½ lb) good stewing beef, cut into 2.5cm (1 in) pieces	salt and freshly ground black pepper
	175g (6 oz) ready-to-eat dried apricots
600g (1 lb 5 oz) shallots, left whole	150ml (¼ pint) port
2 garlic cloves, crushed	chopped fresh parsley to garnish
75g (3 oz) plain flour	

Preheat the oven to 160°C/325°F/Gas 3.

1 Heat the oil in a large, deep frying pan. Brown the venison and beef in batches, adding more oil if necessary. Lift the meat out of the pan, using a slotted spoon. Add the whole shallots and garlic to the pan and cook, stirring occasionally, until evenly browned. Lift out of the pan with a slotted spoon.

2 Lower the heat, then stir the flour into the oil left in the pan, adding more if necessary, and cook for 1 minute. Stir in the stock and red wine and bring to the boil, stirring. Add the redcurrant jelly, and return the meat and shallots to the pan. Season with salt and pepper, bring to the boil, cover, then cook in the preheated oven for 1½ hours.

3 Add the apricots and port to the casserole. Return, covered, to the oven and cook for 1 further hour until the meat is tender. Adjust the seasoning, and stir in lots of parsley to serve.

cook now, eat later

TO PREPARE AND COOK AHEAD Cook the casserole ahead (omitting the parsley), cool quickly, cover and keep in the fridge for up to 2 days. Reheat until piping hot.

TO FREEZE Cool the completed casserole (omitting the parsley). Freeze for up to 2 months. Thaw thoroughly and reheat until piping hot to serve.

TO COOK IN THE AGA Brown the meat on the Boiling Plate. At step 2 cover and transfer to the Simmering Oven for about 2 hours until tender. Follow step 3 and again cover and cook in the Simmering Oven for a further 1–1½ hours or until the meats are tender.

Calf's liver with caramelised onions and balsamic gravy

You can of course fry the onions, but caramelising them in the oven is a bit different! If you can't get calf's liver, use lamb's instead.

Serves 6

700g (1½ lb) calf's liver, thinly sliced (trimmed weight)

plain flour

salt and freshly ground black pepper

40g (1½ oz) butter

CARAMELISED ONIONS

3 large mild onions

olive oil

a little granulated sugar

GRAVY

20g (¾ oz) butter

20g (¾ oz) plain flour

450ml (¾ pint) beef stock

1½ teaspoons soy sauce

1½ dessertspoons balsamic vinegar

a little gravy browning (optional)

Preheat the oven to 220°C/425°F/Gas 7.

1 Peel and thickly slice the onions into rounds 1cm (½ in) thick. Arrange on a well-greased baking sheet. Brush the onion slices with olive oil and a little sugar to caramelise. Cook in the preheated oven for about 30 minutes, turning and seasoning half-way through.

2 Toss the liver in seasoned flour. Heat a non-stick frying pan until very hot then add the butter. Add the liver and cook over a high heat for 1–2 minutes on each side until browned all over and just done in the middle – i.e. no longer showing blood when cut. You may have to do this in two batches. Lift out the liver and keep warm.

3 To make the gravy, melt the butter in a small pan, blend in the flour then add the stock and bring to the boil. Add the soy sauce, balsamic vinegar and some salt and pepper. Add a dash of gravy browning if liked, and check the seasoning.

4 Serve the liver with the caramelised onion rings, balsamic gravy and creamy mashed potatoes.

cook now, eat later

TO PREPARE AND COOK AHEAD Earlier in the day, brown the liver very quickly until golden, about 30 seconds to 1 minute on each side. Lift out, cool, cover and keep in the fridge until needed. Cook the onions in the oven. Set aside. When ready to serve, reheat the liver and the onions in the oven preheated to 220°C/425°F/Gas 7, for about 10 minutes depending upon the thickness of the liver.

TO FREEZE Not suitable.

TO COOK IN THE AGA Cook the onions on a baking sheet on the floor of the Roasting Oven for about 20–25 minutes, turning half-way through, keeping an eye on them. Brown the liver quickly on the Boiling Plate. Reheat towards the top of the Roasting Oven for about 6–7 minutes, depending upon the thickness of the liver. Make the gravy on the Boiling Plate.

VEGETABLES AND SALADS

One usually thinks of a salad as being a last-minute job, but with many salad vegetables you can prepare them – and even dress them – some hours in advance. Here, for instance, the vegetables for the red cabbage salad can be prepared well beforehand, then dressed at least 4 hours before eating. I think you'll agree that that would take quite a lot of the pressure off you if you were busy with other stages of a meal.

But even if you are using more fragile salad vegetables, you can prepare ahead to a certain extent. With something as simple as a green salad, put the dressing in the bottom of the salad bowl, then add the 'tougher', crisper vegetables – shreds of fennel or celery, say, which might benefit from marination. Turn in the dressing, then pile the lettuce leaves on top, but don't stir. Clingfilm the top and put in the fridge for up to 8 hours. The salad will be chilled and crisp when you come to mix it all together, and not soggy from tossing too early. And that's yet another job done.

Vegetables, too, one thinks of as a last-minute thing, and many green vegetables are undeniably best when freshly boiled briefly in salted water. (I do not recommend steaming green vegetables as they lose their bright green colour.) But several dishes can be prepared well in advance and cooked at the last moment. You could part-cook roasted vegetables until golden the day before. I do this with roots mainly – with a mixture as on page 98, or with potatoes and parsnips to go with a roast joint. Then all you have to do on the day is blast them in a very hot oven to get them brown and crisp just before serving.

And, although I haven't given you a recipe here, don't forget about the smart vegetable purée, the ultimate get-ahead dish. It can be boiled, well drained, mashed then seasoned, cream or butter added, up to two days ahead, kept in the fridge, then reheated in the oven in a buttered dish covered with foil. (You're most likely to have the oven on for something else, so the heat isn't crucial.) The favourite purée in our house is celeriac, but you can try carrots, parsnips or a combination.

Chilled Mediterranean Salad **V**

Grainy Mustard and Herb Potato Salad **V**

Pot-roasted Roots with Rosemary **V**

Celeriac and Fresh Herb Salad **V**

Majorcan Tumbet **V**

Red Cabbage with Lemony Coleslaw Dressing **V**

Savoy, Spinach and Leek Stir-fry with a Hint of Orange **V**

Hot Cajun-spiced Potato Wedges **V**

Herbed Fondant Potatoes **V**

Mash Crazy! **V**

For more vegetable and salad ideas, see:

Char-grilled Vegetables with Goat's Cheese (see page 25)

Asparagus and Quail's Egg Salad (see page 32)

Vegetarian Specials section (see page 108)

Three Bean, Tomato and Asparagus Salad (see page 184)

Chilled Mediterranean salad ^V

A colourful salad to enjoy in summer. It's essential that you serve it chilled. It's also good on individual plates as a summer first course, nice with warm bread or rolls.

Serves 6

550g (1¼ lb) ripe tomatoes
(about 6 large)
salt and freshly ground black pepper
1 medium cucumber
1 small mild onion
1 medium red pepper
2 small Little Gem lettuces, broken in
small pieces
2 tablespoons roughly chopped fresh
flat-leaf parsley
leaves from a few sprigs of fresh basil
about 18 black olives (optional)
a few shavings of Parmesan

CROÛTONS
2 slices thick white bread, crust removed
2 tablespoons good olive oil
2 fat garlic cloves, crushed

DRESSING
3 tablespoons good olive oil
1 tablespoon lemon juice
1 teaspoon caster sugar
1 tablespoon balsamic vinegar

1 Slice off the ends of the tomatoes thinly and cut each tomato into 3 slices then slice each round into about 6 wedges. Transfer to a fairly large bowl, season with pepper but don't stir as the tomatoes will break up.

2 Cut the cucumber in half lengthways. Remove the seeds with a melon baller or teaspoon or simply push your thumb nail firmly down the centre of the cucumber from one end to the other. Discard the seeds. Cut the cucumber in slices about the thickness of medium-sliced bread. Add the horseshoe cucumber shapes to the bowl.

3 Peel and cut the onion in 4 then cut each wedge into very fine slices (not cutting through the root) which will fall apart into bow shapes. Add to the bowl.

4 Seed the pepper and cut into fine julienne strips. Add with the lettuce to the bowl but do not mix together. Cover with clingfilm and chill for 6 hours ideally.

5 Meanwhile, make the croûtons and dressing. Cut the bread into rough cubes, and put in a polythene bag with the oil, garlic and a little pepper. Gently shake to evenly coat with the oil. Either put in a foil-lined grill pan and toast under the grill until golden, or brown in a hot oven (about 220°C/425°F/Gas 7), watching carefully.

recipe continued overleaf

6 For the dressing just blend the ingredients in a small bowl, and season with salt and pepper.

7 Take the large bowl from the fridge. Arrange the lettuce as a base for the salad on a serving plate, and add a little salt. Gently toss the rest of the salad in the bowl with the dressing and croûtons and a little salt. Pile on the serving plate and add the parsley, basil, olives and Parmesan.

cook now, eat later

TO PREPARE AND COOK AHEAD Make the salad to the end of step 4 up to 8 hours ahead, and keep in the fridge. The croûtons and dressing can be made a day ahead, no need to chill. Just before the meal shake the dressing, pour over the salad, arrange on the serving plate and garnish.

TO FREEZE Not suitable.

TO COOK IN THE AGA Bake the croûtons on the top set of runners in the Roasting Oven in a foil-lined roasting tin. Watch carefully and turn frequently.

Grainy mustard and herb potato salad ᵛ

Potato salad is always a favourite for a buffet. This is a delicious variation with a slightly lighter dressing.

Serves 6

1 kg (2¼ lb) baby new potatoes	VINAIGRETTE
1 large mild onion, thinly sliced	1½ tablespoons grainy Meaux mustard
salt and freshly ground black pepper	2 tablespoons white wine vinegar
6 tablespoons 'light' low-calorie	1 tablespoon lemon juice
mayonnaise	1 teaspoon caster sugar
2 tablespoons snipped fresh chives	6 tablespoons olive oil
1 tablespoon chopped fresh parsley	

1 Slice the new potatoes in half lengthways. Boil with the onion in salted water for about 15 minutes until just tender. Drain and set aside for about 5 minutes.

2 While the potatoes are cooking, make the vinaigrette. Mix all the ingredients together in a bowl and blend together by hand with a whisk. Season with salt and pepper.

3 When the potatoes have cooled for about 5 minutes (i.e. they are still warm), pour over the vinaigrette, stir and set aside to cool.

4 Mix the mayonnaise and herbs together in a small bowl and mix into the cold potatoes.

cook now, eat later

TO PREPARE AND COOK AHEAD Up to the end of step 3 can be done up to 48 hours ahead. The mayonnaise and herbs can be mixed up to 48 hours in advance but do not mix this with the potatoes until about 10 hours ahead.

TO FREEZE Not suitable.

Pot-roasted roots with rosemary ^V

A prepare-ahead vegetable dish that needs very little last-minute attention. Vary it with other English root vegetables, such as turnips and swede. If you can't get shallots, use small onions, cutting them in half if need be.

Serves 6

350g (12 oz) parsnips, peeled (prepared weight)	350g (12 oz) carrots, peeled (prepared weight)
350g (12 oz) celeriac, peeled (prepared weight)	olive oil
	salt and freshly ground black pepper
350g (12 oz) tiny shallots, peeled and left whole (prepared weight)	a large sprig of fresh rosemary
	chopped fresh parsley

Line a large roasting tin with foil and brush with oil. Preheat the oven to 200°C/400°F/Gas 6.

1 Cut the parsnips and celeriac into neat pieces a similar size to the shallots. Slice the carrots on the diagonal (these should be smaller as they take longer to cook).

2 Bring the vegetables to the boil in salted water to cover, and simmer for 5 minutes. Drain, coat with 2–3 tablespoons of oil and season well.

3 Tip the vegetables into the prepared roasting tin and add the rosemary. Roast in the preheated oven for about 40–50 minutes, turning from time to time, until tender, piping hot, golden brown and crisp.

4 Serve sprinkled with parsley.

cook now, eat later

TO PREPARE AND COOK AHEAD Par-roast the vegetables the day before at step 3 for about 30 minutes, but slightly under-brown. Complete the roasting in a preheated oven at the same temperature for about 30 minutes until piping hot, golden brown and crisp.

TO FREEZE Not suitable.

TO COOK IN THE AGA Cook the vegetables in the roasting tin on the floor of the Roasting Oven for about 40 minutes, turning from time to time, until tender and golden.

Celeriac and fresh herb salad V

Celeriac is a wonderful vegetable, delicious as a purée vegetable accompaniment. It has a thick layer of peel on the outside so it needs to be peeled with a knife not a peeler. It is necessary to blanch the flesh because as soon as cut celeriac is exposed to the air it turns brown. If you prefer a creamy dressing to the light one here, add 4 tablespoons mayonnaise to the dressing.

Serves 6

1 celeriac, weighing about 450g (1 lb)	DRESSING
salt and freshly ground black pepper	juice of 1 lemon
1 large carrot, peeled	4 tablespoons olive oil
	¼ teaspoon caster sugar
	2 tablespoons chopped fresh basil
	2 tablespoons snipped fresh chives
	2 tablespoons chopped fresh parsley

1 Peel and shred the celeriac into very fine strips, about 7.5cm (3 in) long. Blanch the celeriac in boiling salted water for about 1½ minutes, then refresh in cold water, and drain well.

2 Cut the carrot into fine strips about 7.5cm (3 in) long. No need to blanch.

3 Whisk the lemon juice, oil, sugar and some salt and pepper together in a small bowl, then stir in the herbs.

4 Mix the shredded vegetables with the dressing, season with salt and pepper and spoon into a serving dish.

cook now, eat later

TO PREPARE AHEAD Stages 1, 2 and 3 can be prepared up to 48 hours ahead but keep the vegetables separate. The completed dressed salad can be made up to 8 hours ahead.

TO FREEZE Not suitable.

Majorcan tumbet ^V

There is no translation for this classic Majorcan dish. It is a mix of roasted Mediterranean vegetables, potatoes and tomato. My first encounter with it was when we arrived in Majorca to stay with some dear friends. Miranda had made Tumbet with added chicken, and we ate it outside as the sun went down. It's good with barbecues, roast meats, grills or pan-fries. It will keep hot for up to about 40 minutes.

Serves 6

500g (1 lb 2 oz) aubergines	salt and freshly ground black pepper
600g (1 lb 6 oz) baby new potatoes, scrubbed	2 large red peppers, halved and seeded
	olive oil
500g (1 lb 2 oz) Spanish onions, thickly sliced	2 teaspoons chopped fresh rosemary
	400ml (14 fl oz) tomato passata
3 fat garlic cloves, left whole	2 sprigs of fresh thyme

Preheat the oven to 220°C/425°F/Gas 7. You will need an ovenproof dish about 20 × 28 × 5cm (8 × 11 × 2 in), with a capacity of about 1.7 litres (3 pints).

1 First cut the aubergines in half, score them and sprinkle the cut side with a little salt. Leave for about 15 minutes then squeeze to remove the salty juices.

2 Boil the potatoes until not quite done, for about 15–20 minutes, in salted water. Allow to cool enough to handle, then skin and cut in half.

3 Toss the aubergines, onions, whole garlic cloves and peppers in a couple of tablespoons of olive oil, and season well. Arrange cut sides down on a large shallow baking sheet or roasting tin. Roast in the preheated oven until the peppers are charred and the vegetables are soft, about 20–30 minutes, turning once. You may find the peppers take longest, therefore remove the other vegetables, keeping them in separate piles.

4 When the peppers are charred and hot, transfer them to a polythene bag, seal the top and let the peppers sweat and cool in the bag. When cold, peel off the skin.

5 Slice the aubergines into 5mm (¼ in) slices, and cut the peppers into chunky pieces. Squash the garlic with the back of a knife and add the soft flesh to the peppers.

Preheat the oven to 200°C/400°F/Gas 6.

6 Arrange the vegetables in layers in the dish. Layer the potato with seasoning, rosemary and about 6 tablespoons of passata, followed by onion, pepper and aubergine, still with herbs and passata in between each. Push in the sprigs of thyme near the top (these need to be removed to serve).

7 Cook in the hot oven for about 15 minutes (or a lower temperature for longer if it suits you). Remove the sprigs of thyme to serve.

cook now, eat later

TO PREPARE AND COOK AHEAD Prepare to the end of step 6. Cool, and keep in the fridge for up to 3 days. Cook as in step 7, about 15–20 minutes.

TO FREEZE Freeze at the end of step 6. Defrost thoroughly before continuing with step 7, for about 15–20 minutes.

TO COOK IN THE AGA Cook step 3 on the second set of runners in the Roasting Oven for about 20–30 minutes. Cook step 7 directly on the floor of the Roasting Oven for about 15 minutes then slide on to the second set of runners for a further 10 minutes.

TIP Large onions of the Spanish sort have a tough layer of skin directly under the brown skin. It's best to peel this second skin off before using in recipes otherwise it will never soften down, even after long, slow cooking.

Red cabbage with lemony coleslaw dressing V

A variation on a classic coleslaw. There were great discussions here as to whether we liked the colour or not. Some of us loved it, some weren't too sure! It is quite pink, so if you are worried about this, use a white cabbage instead.

Serves 6

1 red cabbage, weighing about 450g (1 lb)	SAUCE
3 small celery sticks	4 tablespoons 'light' low-calorie mayonnaise
2 carrots, peeled	4 tablespoons half-fat crème fraîche
½ mild onion, very finely sliced	juice of 1 lemon
50g (2 oz) walnut pieces (optional)	2 teaspoons Dijon mustard
50g (2 oz) sultanas (optional)	1 teaspoon caster sugar
salt and freshly ground black pepper	2 tablespoons hot water
2 tablespoons chopped fresh parsley	

1 Cut the cabbage into quarters and remove the core. Shred the cabbage, celery and carrots into very fine strips (about 6cm/2½ in long) and add the sliced onion. This can be done in a food processor if preferred. Mix all the vegetables together in a large bowl and stir in the walnuts and sultanas if using them. Season with salt and pepper.

2 Mix the sauce ingredients together in a small bowl until smooth. Pour over the vegetables and mix together, until all the vegetables are coated. Check the seasoning.

3 Mix in the parsley, and turn into a serving dish. Serve at room temperature.

cook now, eat later

TO PREPARE AHEAD All the vegetables can be prepared up to 2 days ahead. The sauce can be made up to 2 days ahead as well, but keep the two separate. Mix together up to 4 hours before serving.

TO FREEZE Not suitable.

Savoy, spinach and leek stir-fry with a hint of orange ᵛ

A quick stir-fry as an alternative vegetable. The orange gives it an out-of-the-ordinary flavour.

Serves 6

450g (1 lb) Savoy cabbage
225g (8 oz) baby spinach
1 large leek
25g (1 oz) butter

finely grated zest and juice of
 1 small orange
salt and freshly ground black pepper

1 First prepare the vegetables. Cut the cabbage into quarters, remove the core and very finely slice. Remove any coarse stalks from the spinach, and wash the leaves if needed. Cut the leek in half lengthways, then in half again, and slice into very thin batons. Wash thoroughly and drain.

2 Melt the butter in a large deep frying pan over a high heat. Stir in the cabbage and leek and stir-fry for about 3–4 minutes. Add the baby spinach, orange zest and juice and season with plenty of salt and pepper, and fry for a further 2 minutes until the spinach has wilted.

3 Pile the vegetables into a warm serving dish and serve at once.

cook now, eat later

TO PREPARE AHEAD All the vegetables can be prepared ahead up to 8 hours before, and kept separately in the fridge.

TO FREEZE Not suitable.

TO COOK IN THE AGA Stir-fry on the Boiling Plate as above.

Hot cajun-spiced potato wedges V

A quick recipe to serve as a snack, or before supper. Good dipped in soured cream or tomato salsa.

Serves 6

2 large potatoes, scrubbed	½ garlic clove, crushed
	½ teaspoon ground coriander
MARINADE	½ teaspoon allspice powder
I tablespoon sunflower oil	½ teaspoon chilli powder
I teaspoon runny honey	salt and freshly ground black pepper

Preheat the oven to 200°C/400°F/Gas 6. Line a small roasting tin with foil or non-stick paper.

1 Cut the potatoes into decent-sized wedges, leaving the skin on. Mix all the marinade ingredients together in a bowl, toss in the potato wedges and mix until well coated. Tip the wedges into the lined roasting tin.

2 Bake in the preheated oven for about 30–40 minutes, giving the tin a little shake half-way through so they do not stick. The potatoes should be cooked through and golden brown and crisp. (The timing depends on the size you cut your potatoes.) Sprinkle with salt and pepper and serve immediately.

3 Serve with a dip made simply from a mixture of soured cream and snipped chives.

cook now, eat later

> **TO PREPARE AHEAD** Prepare the potato wedges in the marinade up to 8 hours ahead.
>
> **TO FREEZE** Not suitable.
>
> **TO COOK IN THE AGA** Slide the tin on the grid shelf on the floor of the Roasting Oven for about 25–30 minutes turning so golden brown all over.

Herbed fondant potatoes ^V

A classic dish, cooking the potatoes simply in butter. The chefs always 'turn' their potatoes into a pretty ridged shape, but I think life is too short for that, so we have sliced them! Do be careful when turning them over so as not to break the potatoes up. The potatoes should not be brown, they should be pale in colour.

Serves 6

1kg (2¼ lb) large King Edward potatoes, peeled	salt and freshly ground black pepper
	1 tablespoon snipped fresh chives
50g (2 oz) butter	1 tablespoon chopped fresh parsley

Preheat the oven to 160°C/325°F/Gas 3.

1 Cut the peeled potatoes into 5mm (¼ in) slices. Melt the butter in a deep non-stick saucepan or casserole dish. Add the potatoes and turn over so they are all coated in the melted butter. Season with salt and pepper, cover with a lid and simmer over a low heat for about 15 minutes.

2 Remove from the heat and cool slightly. Arrange the slices in a shallow 1.2 litre (2 pint) ovenproof dish (no need to butter) so they are overlapping each other. Cover with foil and bake in the preheated oven for about 1½ hours until the potatoes are tender but not coloured.

3 Just before serving sprinkle over the herbs, pushing them between the layers.

cook now, eat later

TO PREPARE AND COOK AHEAD Cook to the end of step 1, arrange in the ovenproof dish, and put in the fridge up to 12 hours ahead. To reheat, bring to room temperature and continue with steps 2 and 3.

TO FREEZE Not suitable.

TO COOK IN THE AGA Cook step 1 on the Simmering Plate for about 10 minutes. Arrange in overlapping slices in an ovenproof dish, cover with foil and put on the grid shelf on the floor of the Roasting Oven for about 10 minutes. Transfer to the Simmering Oven for a further 1½ hours.

Mash crazy! ^V

One of the world's favourite potato dishes is mash, and there are so many flavours you can use that we thought we would give you a choice! Remember to think of the dishes you are serving the mash with, so that the flavours complement each other.

Boil peeled cubed potatoes in boiling salted water until tender. Drain, add milk and butter, salt and pepper, and mash until mixed, then beat with a hand whisk until smooth and creamy. Choose from the list below and stir in at the end to make the mash extra special! For each kg (2¼ lb) potatoes – to serve 4–6 – add:

Grainy Mustard Mash

About 3 tablespoons grainy mustard.

Leek Mash

You will need 2 good-sized leeks, sliced and white parts boiled with the potatoes. Add the very finely sliced green parts for the last 5 minutes.

Potato and Parsnip Mash

Boil 500g (1 lb 2 oz) parsnips with the potatoes.

Sweet Potato Mash

On its own, using sweet potatoes instead of ordinary.

Creamy Horseradish Mash

Add about 4–5 tablespoons creamed horseradish (only 2 for the hot horseradish!).

Spring Onion Mash

Slice a small bunch of spring onions finely. Boil the white parts with the potatoes and add the green parts at the end.

Potato and Celeriac Mash

Boil equal quantities of celeriac with the potatoes.

Mediterranean Mash

Add about 3 tablespoons olive oil, 50g (2 oz) chopped black olives and
8 chopped sun-dried tomatoes to the mash.

Fresh Herb and Garlic Mash

Add a small bunch each of chopped fresh parsley and chives and
2 fat crushed garlic cloves to the mash.

Mature Cheddar Mash

Add about 75g (3 oz) coarsely grated mature Cheddar to the mash.

Red or Green Pesto Mash

Add about 3 tablespoons bought or home-made red or green pesto to the mash.

cook now, eat later

TO PREPARE AND COOK AHEAD Mashed potato is best served straightaway, but if you wish to do it some hours ahead, quickly cool the mash, and check the seasoning. Well butter a shallow ovenproof dish large enough to give a layer of 5 cm (2 in). Roughly fork over the top and add a few knobs of butter. Blast in a very hot oven at 220°C/425°F/Gas 7 for about 20 minutes. Serve immediately.

TO FREEZE Not suitable.

TO COOK IN THE AGA If reheating the mash in the dish, do so on the top set of runners in the Roasting Oven.

VEGETARIAN SPECIALS

I have included this section – as I have done in many of my previous books – because our youngest, Annabel, is vegetarian, as are many of her friends. We have really enjoyed cooking with beans, lentils and chickpeas, and have discovered how good most of the pulses available in cans are. All you need to do is open the can and rinse the contents! However, if I were cooking for a big event, I would always use dried pulses – soaking and cooking them – primarily because of the cost factor. But for small quantities, I heartily recommend tinned beans and chickpeas. So far as lentils are concerned, I like the French Puy, which are full of flavour themselves, but also absorb flavour from other ingredients while cooking. Couscous is also a wonderful ingredient. It gives texture to a dish and is perfect for use as a stuffing. When serving on the side, season and flavour it well with herbs and finely chopped fresh vegetables (see pages 76 or 124).

Flavour is perhaps the most vital element in vegetarian dishes. Although vegetables, pulses and grains are full of their own individual flavours, these are not strong, and need to be helped along by herbs, spices and often the vegetarian stand-by of cheese. Texture and colour are important too, so add crispness if you can in the form of a bit of celery or spring onion, and enliven the look of a dish with the bright colours of sweet peppers or fresh herbs.

You will notice that most of the recipes here are the vegetarian equivalent of conventional meat dishes. Most are now considered 'comfort' foods, and I wouldn't want vegetarians to miss out on those! I have not used meat substitutes, but the combinations of vegetables we have used make for a wonderful moussaka, cottage pie, lasagne and even sausages. Many vegetarian recipes can be cooked in advance, but the majority here – from a taste and texture point of view – are prepared well ahead and then cooked at the last minute. But with all that chopping, cutting, seeding, trimming and peeling out of the way, you will find cooking vegetarian very easy indeed!

Spinach and Feta Frittata **V**

Bean Bangers **V**

Stir-fried Vegetable Lasagne **V**

Spiced Lentil and Tomato Moussaka **V**

Lentil and Vegetable Cottage Pie **V**

Chunky Vegetable Thai Curry **V**

Herb Falafels **V**

Onion, Apple and Stilton Little Quiches **V**

Mediterranean Vegetable Galette with Mozzarella **V**

Roasted Field Mushrooms with Couscous and Feta **V**

Parisian Red Peppers **V**

For more vegetarian ideas, see:

Winter Vegetable Soup (see page 16)

The Very Best Porcini Mushroom Soup (see page 17)

Butternut Squash Soup (see page 18)

Char-grilled Vegetables with Goat's Cheese (see page 25)

Twice-baked Tomato and Feta Soufflés (see page 34)

Vegetables and Salads section (see page 92)

Chilled Mediterranean Salad (see page 94)

Pasta Primavera (see page 131)

Pistou Pasta with Rocket (see page 134)

Three Bean, Tomato and Asparagus Salad (see page 184)

Spinach and feta frittata ᵛ

A frittata is a baked omelette, finished under the grill. Like an omelette, a frittata should not be overcooked. It is ideal for a light supper or for lunch. Serve with crusty bread and a salad.

Serves 6

6 eggs	100g (4 oz) closed-cup mushrooms
4 tablespoons milk	100g (4 oz) fresh baby spinach, coarsely
salt and freshly ground black pepper	sliced
a little freshly grated nutmeg	75g (3 oz) feta cheese, diced
a knob of butter	25g (1 oz) black olives in oil, drained and
1 tablespoon sunflower oil	halved
8 spring onions, sliced on the diagonal	a handful of fresh basil leaves, torn

1 Blend together the eggs and milk in a bowl. Season with salt, pepper and nutmeg.

2 Melt the butter and oil in a large non-stick frying pan and fry the spring onions and mushrooms over a high heat for a couple of minutes. Add the spinach, stir for 1 minute, then season.

3 Pour the egg mixture into the pan and spread the spinach and mushroom mixture out through the egg. Sprinkle over the feta cheese and olives.

4 Cook over a medium heat, loosening the edge with a spatula, for about 5–6 minutes until the base and edges of the mixture are set. Place under a preheated grill for a further 3–4 minutes or until the top is just set and golden brown.

5 Invert the frittata on to a heated serving plate, cut into wedges and garnish with basil.

cook now, eat later

TO PREPARE AND COOK AHEAD Prepare all the vegetables the day before, arrange on a plate in groups, cover with clingfilm and put in the fridge. Then the frittata will only take minutes to make. Or cook the frittata completely, turn out and allow to cool. Serve cold, cut into wedges for a summer lunch or picnic. Best made the same day, and not chilled.

TO FREEZE Not suitable.

TO COOK IN THE AGA Cook step 2 on the Boiling Plate. At step 3, transfer to the grid shelf on the second set of runners in the Roasting Oven for about 4–6 minutes until just set.

Bean bangers ^V

It is best to shape these sausages so that they are fairly short and fat rather than long and thin. They are then easier to cook, and won't break up.

Serves 6

½ red onion, finely chopped

2 tablespoons chopped fresh parsley

1 teaspoon chopped fresh thyme

1 × 410g can cannellini beans, drained and rinsed

1 × 300g can red kidney beans, drained and rinsed

50g (2 oz) sun-dried tomatoes, coarsely chopped

50g (2 oz) Cheddar or mozzarella cheese, grated

2 tablespoons beaten egg

salt and freshly ground black pepper

50g (2 oz) fresh breadcrumbs

2–3 tablespoons olive oil

1 Put the onion, parsley and thyme into a food processor and purée until fairly smooth. Add all the remaining ingredients except the breadcrumbs and oil to the processor and process until smooth.

2 Shape the mixture into 12 sausages. Put the breadcrumbs on a large plate then roll the sausages in them to coat evenly. Chill in the fridge for 30 minutes.

3 Heat the oil in a large frying pan and brown the sausages until golden, turning carefully so that they do not break up. Lower the heat and continue to cook until the sausages are hot right through.

cook now, eat later

TO PREPARE AHEAD Prepare the sausages up to the end of step 2. Cover and keep in the fridge for up to 24 hours. Continue with step 3. You can also brown the sausages and reheat in a hot oven.

TO FREEZE Not suitable.

TO COOK IN THE AGA Brown the sausages in a frying pan on the Boiling Plate until golden then transfer to a baking sheet and place on the second set of runners in the Roasting Oven for about 7–10 minutes until firm.

Stir-fried vegetable lasagne ^V

There is no lengthy sauce-making process for this lasagne. The 'sauce' is simply mascarpone and ricotta cheeses mixed together with single cream and plenty of seasoning. It is fairly rich so only needs to be spread thinly for each layer.

Serves 6

3 tablespoons olive oil	2 tablespoons chopped fresh parsley
2 large onions, roughly chopped	salt and freshly ground black pepper
3 garlic cloves, crushed	100g (4 oz) Emmental cheese, grated
350g (12 oz) chestnut mushrooms, sliced	150g (5 oz) dried pre-cooked lasagne
1 aubergine, cut into sugar-cube-sized pieces	50g (2 oz) Parmesan, freshly grated
1 red pepper, seeded and roughly chopped	QUICK SAUCE
1 tablespoon plain flour	1 × 250g tub mascarpone cheese
1 × 400g can chopped tomatoes	1 × 250g tub ricotta cheese
	300ml (½ pint) single cream

Preheat the oven to 190°C/375°F/Gas 5. You will need a shallow ovenproof dish about 25.5 × 23cm (10 × 9 in).

1 Heat the oil in a large frying pan, add the onions and garlic, and cook over a high heat, stirring from time to time, for about 4–5 minutes. Add the mushrooms, aubergine and red pepper and cook, stirring still over a high heat, for 2–3 minutes. Lower the heat, cover the pan and cook for about 20 minutes, until the aubergine is tender.

2 Blend the flour with the juices from the can of tomatoes in a bowl, and mix until smooth. Add with the tomatoes, parsley and seasoning to the vegetable mixture, and stir well. Cover again and simmer for a further 10–15 minutes. Check the seasoning.

3 For the sauce, simply mix together the mascarpone and ricotta cheeses with the cream and season well with salt and pepper.

4 To assemble, spread one-third of the mushroom and aubergine mixture over the base, then one-third of the sauce and a third of the Emmental. Cover with a single layer of half the lasagne sheets and then repeat these layers twice more, sandwiching the remaining pasta. Finish the top with the Parmesan.

5 Cook in the preheated oven for about 40 minutes until the top is golden and bubbling, and the lasagne is piping hot. Serve with crusty bread and a fresh green salad.

TO PREPARE AND COOK AHEAD Complete to the end of stage 4. Cool, cover and keep in the fridge for up to 2 days. Cook as in step 5, but for a little longer, about 50 minutes.

TO FREEZE Freeze the dish prepared up to the end of step 4, well wrapped, for up to a month. To thaw, defrost in the fridge overnight, and cook as in step 5, but for a little longer, about 50 minutes.

TO COOK IN THE AGA Cook the onions and garlic on the Boiling Plate. Add the mushrooms, aubergine and red pepper, cover and transfer to the Simmering Oven for 25 minutes. Blend in the flour, tomatoes, parsley and seasoning, bring to the boil, cover and return to the Simmering Oven for about 10–15 minutes. Complete steps 3 and 4 then cook on the second set of runners in the Roasting Oven for about 35–45 minutes until cooked through and golden brown.

Spiced lentil and tomato moussaka V

You need not be a vegetarian to enjoy this dish. It is rich in flavour and, with the added red peppers and tomatoes, colourful too. Buy dried French Puy lentils in packets, and add as they are.

Serves 6

6 tablespoons olive oil
2 large onions, roughly chopped
3 large garlic cloves, crushed
2 large red peppers, seeded and
   chopped into large pieces
225g (8 oz) dried Puy lentils
3 × 400g cans chopped tomatoes
300ml (½ pint) vegetable stock
1–2 tablespoons mango chutney
salt and freshly ground black pepper
3 large aubergines, thickly sliced,
   about 5mm (¼ in)

CHEESE SAUCE
50g (2 oz) butter
50g (2 oz) plain flour
600ml (1 pint) milk
225g (8 oz) mature Cheddar, grated
2 teaspoons Dijon mustard
freshly grated nutmeg to taste

Preheat the oven to 200°C/400°F/Gas 6, and lightly grease a large, shallow, ovenproof dish, about 25 × 33cm (10 × 13 in).

1 Heat 2 tablespoons of the olive oil in a large sauté pan. Add the onions, garlic and peppers and cook gently for about 4–5 minutes until beginning to soften.

2 Add the lentils, tomatoes, vegetable stock, mango chutney and seasoning. Cover and simmer for about 40–60 minutes or until the lentils are cooked. Check the seasoning.

3 Brush the sliced aubergines with the remaining olive oil and season with salt and pepper. Arrange in a single layer (you will have to do this in batches) on a baking sheet and place under a hot grill for about 2–3 minutes each side, until the slices are golden brown.

4 Next make the cheese sauce. Melt the butter in a medium saucepan, take off the heat and stir in the flour. Return to a low heat, stirring for 2–3 minutes, then again remove from the heat and gradually add the milk. Bring up to the boil, stirring, and simmer for about 2 minutes. Add 175g (6 oz) of the cheese, the mustard, nutmeg and some salt and pepper.

recipe continued overleaf

5 To assemble the moussaka, spoon half of the lentil mixture into the dish, cover with half of the cheese sauce and arrange half of the aubergine slices on top. Repeat with the remaining lentil mixture, cheese sauce and aubergine. Sprinkle the remaining grated cheese on top of the aubergine.

6 Cook in the oven for about 30–40 minutes or until golden on top and piping hot. Serve with crusty bread and a fresh green salad.

cook now, eat later

TO PREPARE AND COOK AHEAD Assemble the moussaka as in step 5, but don't cook in the oven yet. Cool, cover and keep in the fridge for up to 1 day. Cook from room temperature in the oven at the same temperature as above for 40–50 minutes until golden on top and piping hot right through.

TO FREEZE Cover and freeze the assembled, but not oven-cooked, moussaka for up to 3 months. Thaw overnight in the fridge. Cook as above.

TO COOK IN THE AGA Cook the lentils to the end of step 2 in the Simmering Oven for about 1¼ hours. Cook the aubergines on the highest set of runners in the Roasting Oven, 3–5 minutes each side. Make the sauce on the Simmering Plate. Cook the assembled dish on the grid shelf on the floor of the Roasting Oven for about 30–40 minutes.

Lentil and vegetable cottage pie ᵛ

This idea was very popular when we were trying it out. It is cheap to produce, and tastes delicious!

Serves 6

2 large onions, finely chopped	50g (2 oz) sun-dried tomatoes, drained if
2 garlic cloves, crushed	in oil, and chopped
2 tablespoons olive oil	salt and freshly ground black pepper
3 celery sticks, sliced	
2 large carrots, sliced	
100g (4 oz) dried red lentils, rinsed	TOPPING
1 × 400g can chopped tomatoes	1kg (2¼ lb) old potatoes, peeled
300ml (½ pint) vegetable stock	about 150ml (¼ pint) milk
2 teaspoons sun-dried tomato paste	a bunch of spring onions, finely chopped
	25g (1 oz) butter
	175g (6 oz) mature Cheddar, grated

Preheat the oven to 200°C/400°F/Gas 6. You will need an ovenproof dish, about 28 × 23 × 5cm (11 × 9 × 2 in).

1 Cook the onions and garlic in the oil over a low heat in a large pan for about 10 minutes until soft. Add the celery and carrots and cook for a further 5 minutes. Stir in the lentils, then add the chopped tomatoes, stock, tomato paste, sun-dried tomatoes and plenty of seasoning. Bring to the boil, cover and simmer for about 20 minutes until the vegetables are tender. Check the seasoning.

2 Meanwhile, cook the potatoes in boiling salted water until tender. Whilst the potatoes are cooking, heat the milk and spring onions together in a small pan and simmer gently for about 5 minutes until the spring onions are soft. Drain the potatoes well, then add the warm milk with the spring onions and the butter. Mash together adding plenty of salt and pepper. Stir in two-thirds of the grated cheese and check the seasoning.

3 Spoon the vegetable mixture into the prepared dish and gently spread the potato on top. Scatter the remaining cheese over the top of the potato.

4 Cook in the preheated oven for about 30 minutes until the potato is golden and the sauce bubbling.

cook now, eat later

TO PREPARE AND COOK AHEAD Make ahead to the end of step 3 but don't put into the oven. Cool, cover and keep in the fridge for up to 24 hours. Complete step 4 to serve, cooking for about 40 minutes.

TO FREEZE Not suitable.

TO COOK IN THE AGA Cook the onions, etc. firstly on the Boiling Plate, then transfer, covered, to the Simmering Oven for 30 minutes or until tender. Cook the potatoes on the Boiling Plate. Cook the assembled dish on a high shelf in the Roasting Oven for about 20 minutes until golden brown and piping hot.

Chunky vegetable Thai curry ^V

A delicious vegetable curry suitable for non meat-eaters.

Serves 6

2 tablespoons sunflower oil	450ml (¾ pint) vegetable stock
1 large onion, chopped into large pieces	1 × 400ml can coconut milk
2 fat garlic cloves, crushed	salt and freshly ground black pepper
1 fat small green chilli, seeded and chopped	175g (6 oz) runner beans, in 1cm (½ in) pieces
about 2.5cm (1 in) piece root ginger, grated	100g (4 oz) large-cup mushrooms, quartered
finely grated zest of ½ lime	½ red pepper, seeded and thinly sliced
1 tablespoon ground coriander	100g (4 oz) baby sweetcorn, cut lengthways
1 tablespoon ground cumin	1 × 400g can flageolet beans, drained
1 tablespoon garam masala	and rinsed
175g (6 oz) sweet potatoes, cut into batons	juice of 1 lime
175g (6 oz) parsnips, cut into batons	fresh coriander leaves

1 Heat the oil in a large, deep frying pan and fry the onion for about 10 minutes over a low heat until starting to soften. Add the garlic, chilli, ginger and lime zest to the onion and stir-fry for 2–3 minutes. Add the spices, mix in well and cook for 1 minute over a high heat.

2 Peel the sweet potatoes and parsnips, blend in the stock and coconut milk and season with salt and pepper. Bring to the boil, stirring, cover and simmer over a low heat for about 10–15 minutes until the vegetables are nearly tender. Blanch the runner beans in a pan of boiling salted water for about 4 minutes until al dente. Drain and refresh in cold water until completely cold. Set aside to dry.

3 Add the mushrooms, red pepper, sweetcorn, flageolet beans and dry, blanched runner beans to the pan, stir well and bring back to the boil for 1 minute. Cover and continue to cook over a low heat for a further 10–15 minutes until all the vegetables are tender. Check the seasoning, add the lime juice and coriander and serve with rice.

cook now, eat later

TO PREPARE AND COOK AHEAD Steps 1 and 2 can be done up to 12 hours ahead.

TO FREEZE Not suitable.

TO COOK IN THE AGA Soften onion for 10 minutes, covered in Simmering Oven. Continue with steps 1 and 2, bring to boil on Boiling Plate, and transfer to Simmering Oven for 10 minutes until the vegetables are tender. Follow step 3, cover and transfer to Simmering Oven for a further 10–15 minutes until tender.

Herb falafels ᵛ

A quick and easy supper dish, and the falafels can be made in any shape or size you like. For a starter, little tiny ones look very effective.

Serves 6

2 × 410g cans chickpeas, drained	1½ tablespoons olive oil
2 teaspoons ground cumin	salt and freshly ground black pepper
1 teaspoon ground turmeric	
1 teaspoon cayenne pepper	TO FINISH
1 garlic clove, crushed	a little plain flour for coating
½ bunch fresh coriander, leaves and stalks	a little vegetable oil for frying

1 Measure all the falafel ingredients, except for the olive oil and seasoning, into a food processor. Process until blended, but still with a coarse texture. Add the olive oil and process again to mix. Season with salt and pepper.

2 Shape into 12 ovals about 7.5cm (3 in) long and 1cm (½ in) deep. Transfer to the fridge for at least 1 hour, if time allows, to firm up.

3 Coat with a little flour ready for frying.

4 Heat a frying pan until very hot, add a little oil and fry the falafels for about 5 minutes on each side until golden brown and hot right through. Transfer to kitchen paper for a moment before serving.

5 Serve immediately with fresh yogurt and mint, and a herby green salad.

cook now, eat later

TO PREPARE AND COOK AHEAD After step 2, the falafels can be put into the fridge up to 24 hours ahead. Then follow step 3 onwards to cook and serve. Or, cool after step 4 and put in the fridge up to 24 hours ahead. Either quickly fry them to reheat, or put in a hot oven at 200°C/400°F/Gas 6 for about 10–15 minutes.

TO FREEZE Not suitable.

TO COOK IN THE AGA Cook in a hot frying pan on the Boiling Plate. If cooked in advance, reheat on a baking sheet on the floor of the Roasting Oven for about 10 minutes until piping hot.

Onion, apple and Stilton little quiches ᵛ

A delicious variation on an old favourite of ours, the apple and sage giving a wonderfully unusual flavour. Make these in two 4-portion Yorkshire pudding tins, each making 4 individual tarts. This pastry is really cheesy and delicious, so well worth making if you have time. If time is short, use bought shortcrust pastry instead of home-made.

Makes 8

HERB AND CHEESE PASTRY	FILLING
175g (6 oz) plain flour	1 tablespoon olive oil
½ teaspoon salt	1 large Spanish onion, thinly sliced
1 teaspoon mustard powder	100g (4 oz) cooking apple, peeled and
75g (3 oz) butter, cut into small pieces	coarsely grated
1 teaspoon chopped fresh sage	½ teaspoon sugar
50g (2 oz) Parmesan, freshly grated	100g (4 oz) Stilton cheese, grated
1 large egg, beaten	2 large eggs
	scant 200ml (⅓ pint) double cream
	salt and freshly ground black pepper
	1 teaspoon coarsely chopped fresh sage

1 First make the pastry. Measure the flour, salt, mustard, butter and sage into the food processor or a bowl, and process or rub in until the mixture resembles fine breadcrumbs. Add the Parmesan and the beaten egg and mix again just for as long as it takes for the ingredients to come together. Chill for 30 minutes wrapped in clingfilm.

2 For the filling, heat the oil in a pan and cook the onion over a high heat for a few minutes. Cover and cook over a low heat until soft, about 10–15 minutes. Return to a high heat, add the apple and fry for a further 5 minutes, stirring all the time. Add the sugar, and cook for a few minutes without the lid to evaporate any liquid from the onion. Cool.

3 Roll the pastry thinly on a lightly floured work surface and using a 11.5cm (4¾ in) cutter, cut out 8 discs. Use these to line 2 × 4-hole Yorkshire pudding trays. Chill if time allows.

Preheat the oven to 220°C/425°F/Gas 7. Put 2 baking sheets into the oven to heat.

4 Divide the cold onion and apple between the tartlet cases, and top with the Stilton. Beat the eggs and add the cream and seasoning. Carefully pour the egg and cream mixture into the tartlets, then sprinkle evenly with sage. Put the Yorkshire pudding tins on top of the preheated baking sheets. Bake for about 15–20 minutes until the tarts are set and pale golden.

5 Serve warm as a first course or a light lunch with salad. Serves 8 – so 2 for lunch the next day if you are just 6!

cook now, eat later

TO PREPARE AND COOK AHEAD Make the pastry up to 1 day ahead, and line the tins. Cook the apple and onion. Cool and divide between the tarts, add the Stilton, cover and keep in the fridge up to 8 hours ahead. Pour in the cream and egg and sprinkle with the sage just before cooking. The quichelets can also be cooked ahead completely, and reheated to serve in the oven preheated to 200°C/400°F/Gas 6 for about 10 minutes. Keep an eye on them.

TO FREEZE The cooked quichelets freeze well. Cool, wrap, and freeze for up to 3 months. Thaw for about 4 hours at room temperature and reheat to serve as above.

TO COOK IN THE AGA Cook the filling as in step 2, covered, in the Simmering Oven, for about 15–20 minutes. Bake the assembled tarts on the grid shelf on the floor of the Roasting Oven for 15–20 minutes, turning around half-way through the cooking time, until set and pale golden. If the pastry is not brown underneath put the tins directly on the floor of the oven for a few minutes.

Mediterranean vegetable galette with mozzarella V

A delicious puff pastry case filled with stir-fried vegetables. Ready-rolled puff pastry is easy to buy and even easier to use! The pastry border around the edge will rise up and frame the vegetables like a picture. It is essential to preheat the baking sheet as the bottom heat is needed to brown the pastry underneath the vegetables.

Serves 6

1 × 375g (13 oz) packet ready-rolled puff pastry	1 red pepper and 1 yellow pepper, seeded and cut into 2.5cm (1 in) cubes
1 egg, beaten	
fresh basil	1 small garlic clove, crushed
	salt and freshly ground black pepper
FILLING	100g (4 oz) Philadelphia full-fat cream cheese
1 tablespoon olive oil	
1 small aubergine, cut in half lengthways and thinly sliced	1 tablespoon pesto
	50g (2 oz) cherry tomatoes, halved
1 red onion, finely sliced	75g (3 oz) mozzarella cheese, coarsely grated

Preheat the oven to 220°C/425°F/Gas 7. Put a large heavy baking sheet on a high shelf in the oven to preheat.

1 Heat the oil in a deep frying pan, and stir-fry the aubergine until golden brown. Add the onion, peppers and garlic, and continue to stir-fry for about 5–10 minutes until the peppers are just cooked. Make sure that all the moisture has been driven off, over a high heat if necessary, otherwise the pastry will be soggy. Season with salt and pepper. Set aside to cool.

2 Take the ready-rolled puff pastry and roll out a little bigger to a fairly thin rectangle – about 25.5 × 38cm (10 × 15 in). Transfer to a hot baking sheet and score a 4cm (1½ in) border around the edge of the rectangle (score with a knife half-way through the pastry, do not cut right through). Using a sharp knife, diagonally mark around the border about every inch to give a pretty edge (again, do not cut right through). Prick the base of the pastry inside the border.

3 Mix the cream cheese in a bowl with the pesto and season with salt and pepper. Spread the cream cheese mixture evenly over the raw pastry, inside the marked border. Pile the cooled, cooked vegetables over the top of the cream cheese (again ensuring all is inside the border). Arrange the tomatoes (cut side up) on top of the vegetables and scatter over the mozzarella. Brush the pastry border with a little beaten egg.

recipe continued overleaf

4 Take the baking sheet out of the oven and quickly slide the foil with the galette on top on to the hot baking sheet. Return to the oven and bake for 20–25 minutes or until the pastry rises around the vegetables and is a good golden brown. Scatter with basil, and serve with a fresh green salad.

cook now, eat later

TO PREPARE AND COOK AHEAD Cook the vegetables ahead. Cool, cover and keep in the fridge for up to 1 day. Roll and mark the pastry. Cover and keep in the fridge for 1 day. Mix the cheese and pesto, cover and keep in the fridge for up to 1 day. Assemble just before baking.

TO FREEZE Not suitable.

TO COOK IN THE AGA Cook the vegetables on the Boiling Plate. The galette can be cooked on non-stick paper or a greased baking sheet (no need to preheat the baking sheet). Slide the baking sheet directly on to the floor of the Roasting Oven for about 10–15 minutes or until the pastry rises around the vegetables and the base starts to brown. Transfer to the second set of runners of the Roasting Oven for about 8–10 minutes until the pastry is golden brown and the cheese is brown and crisp.

Roasted field mushrooms with couscous and feta ^V

If you are keen on goat's cheese, use that instead of the feta. Choose a firm goat's cheese which can be cut into cubes. Serve with a mixed salad.

Serves 6

12 large flat mushrooms	1 garlic clove, crushed
2–3 tablespoons olive oil	225g (8 oz) couscous
a knob of butter	300ml (½ pint) vegetable stock
salt and freshly ground black pepper	400g (14 oz) feta cheese, cubed
3 very large tomatoes, each sliced into 4 thick slices	about 3 tablespoons chopped fresh parsley, plus more to garnish
1 medium onion, finely chopped	

Preheat the oven to 200°C/400°F/Gas 6.

1 Remove the central stalks from the mushrooms. Heat half the oil in a large frying pan, add the butter and cook the mushrooms lightly, turning until nearly tender. You will have to do this in a couple of batches, depending on the size of your pan. Remove the mushrooms to a large shallow ovenproof dish (or two smaller dishes), large enough to hold the mushrooms in a single layer. Season with salt and pepper.

2 Lightly fry the 12 thick slices of tomato, season and put on top of the mushrooms.

3 Heat the remaining oil in the pan. Add the onion and garlic and cook until soft, about 10 minutes.

4 Meanwhile, measure the couscous into a bowl, pour over the boiling stock and leave to soak until all the stock has been absorbed. Add the cooked onion and garlic to the couscous, lightly stir in the cheese cubes and parsley and season (go easy on the salt as the feta is salty). Divide between the mushrooms in the dish.

5 Cook in the preheated oven for about 20–30 minutes until hot through and the cheese cubes are tinged with brown and bubbling. Scatter with more parsley to serve.

cook now, eat later

TO PREPARE AND COOK AHEAD Prepare to the end of step 4. Cover and keep in the fridge for up to 24 hours. Cook as above in step 5.

TO FREEZE Not suitable.

TO COOK IN THE AGA Fry the mushrooms in a pan on the Boiling Plate for a couple of minutes on each side. Remove to an ovenproof dish. Add the slices of tomato to the pan and cook for 1 minute. Put on to the mushrooms. Follow step 4. Bake on the second set of runners in the Roasting Oven for about 15–20 minutes until tinged with brown.

TIP Try to always have some chopped fresh parsley in the fridge, as it makes all the difference to the look of a dish such as a white fish recipe or pale soup. Pack into a mug tightly covered with clingfilm, with a couple of holes pierced in the top, and it will keep fresh for a good few days.

Parisian red peppers V

Ideal for a light lunch. Serve with crusty bread to soak up the juices and perhaps a green salad. Mozzarella can be used instead of halloumi.

Serves 6

6 large red peppers

salt and freshly ground black pepper

2 tablespoons olive oil

1 medium onion, finely chopped

1 garlic clove, crushed

225g (8 oz) chestnut mushrooms, sliced

2 × 300g cans flageolet beans, rinsed and drained

about 24 black olives, stoned

about 2 tablespoons roughly chopped fresh basil

2 × 250g packs halloumi cheese, coarsely grated

fresh basil leaves to garnish

Preheat the oven to 180°C/350°F/Gas 4. Lightly oil a large, shallow ovenproof dish, large enough to fit 12 pepper halves snugly in a single layer (or two smaller shallow dishes).

1 Cut the peppers in half lengthways, leaving the green stalk but removing the seeds. Put into the ovenproof dish and season lightly.

2 Heat the oil in a medium pan, add the onion and garlic and cook gently for 5–10 minutes until soft. Add the mushrooms and continue to cook until tender. Add the beans and olives to the pan and season to taste.

3 Divide the bean and mushroom mixture between the pepper halves, scatter with the chopped basil and top with the cheese.

4 Bake in the preheated oven for about 1 hour until the peppers are tender and the cheese golden and bubbling. Scatter with basil leaves to serve.

cook now, eat later

TO PREPARE AND COOK AHEAD Cook and cool the mushroom and bean mixture, then use to fill the peppers. Complete step 3, cover and keep in the fridge for up to 8 hours.

TO FREEZE Not suitable.

TO COOK IN THE AGA Cook the onion and mushrooms on the Boiling Plate. Loosely cover the assembled dish with foil, and slide on to the grid shelf on the floor of the Roasting Oven for about 30 minutes. Remove the foil and cook for a further 20 minutes or until the peppers are tender and the cheese golden and bubbling.

SUPPER DISHES

I included this section because I think a good number of people these days prefer to eat in the kitchen with friends rather than give more formal dinner parties. And of course, when people are milling around you in the kitchen – chatting, laughing, perhaps even trying to help (or interfering!) – you want to be as well organised and as well ahead as possible. You don't want your knife technique to come under criticism, or any unwashed pots to be too much in evidence.

Even if you are offering something that must be cooked at the last moment, you can have prepared part of it beforehand. I've suggested a few pasta recipes here – comfort food, always welcomed by guests of all ages – and, perhaps surprisingly, the pasta can be cooked up to 6 hours in advance. I always use dried pasta when I plan to do this. (In fact I believe the Italians prefer dried pasta to fresh, and that's good enough for me!) What you do is cook the pasta in plenty of boiling salted water until al dente, still with a slight bite in the centre. Refresh in plenty of cold running water. Leave the cold pasta in the colander, and cover with clingfilm. To reheat, either tip the pasta into the hot sauce if the pasta has a sauce with it, or plunge into boiling salted water for a few moments, stirring until the pasta is piping hot. Drain and serve at once.

Foods that need to be crisp should be done at the last moment, but the vegetables for the *Phad Thai Noodles* (see page 138), for instance, can be prepared well ahead, as can the marination of the fajita filling. A bit of stir-frying isn't going to prove too difficult in front of your guests. But otherwise the remainder of the recipes here can be prepared and cooked at least a day before, and then reheated, which allows you to mingle happily with your guests, share a drink with them, and enjoy the evening without any hassle in the kitchen.

Pasta Primavera **V**

Chilli-hot Monkfish Pasta with Vegetables

Penne Pasta with Parma Ham

Pistou Pasta with Rocket **V**

Salmon Coulibiac

Phad Thai Noodles with Seafood

Spicy Turkey Fajitas

Turkey Salad with Avocado, Bacon and Pesto Dressing

Piquant Chicken with Basil

Aromatic Thai Rice **V**

Thai Pork Curry

Baked Sausages with Double Onion Marmalade

For more supper ideas, see:

Individual Baked Artichoke and Parma Ham Galettes (see page 26)

Crab Cakes with Mild Chilli Sauce (see page 30)

Twice-baked Tomato and Feta Soufflés (see page 34)

Double Haddock and Herb Fish Cakes (see page 39)

Moroccan Fish (see page 52)

Chardonnay Chicken with Artichoke Hearts (see page 62)

Chicken Olives Provençal (see page 66)

Mexican Spicy Lamb (see page 80)

Tagine of Lamb (see page 83)

Pork Escalopes with Apple and Onion (see page 84)

Onion, Apple and Stilton Little Quiches (see page 120)

See also Vegetarian Specials (pages 108–127)

Pasta primavera ^V

A fresh, fairly healthy – and meat-free – pasta recipe, using bright, colourful vegetables.

Serves 6

2 tablespoons olive oil	350g (12 oz) dried tagliatelle
2 large onions, halved and thickly sliced	225g (8 oz) broccoli florets
2 red peppers, seeded and cut into	225g (8 oz) asparagus tips
large pieces	200ml (7 fl oz) crème fraîche
salt and freshly ground black pepper	3–4 tablespoons pesto, according
350g (12 oz) small courgettes,	to taste
thickly sliced	50g (2 oz) Parmesan, freshly grated

Preheat the oven to 220°C/425°F/Gas 7.

1 Measure the oil into a large polythene bag, add the onions and red peppers and season well. Toss together, then turn into a large roasting tin and roast in the preheated oven, turning from time to time, for about 40 minutes, until the vegetables are just done. Add the courgettes after 20 minutes as they take less time to cook.

2 Boil the pasta in salted water according to the instructions on the packet, usually about 10 minutes, adding the broccoli and asparagus for the last 3 minutes. Drain and leave in the colander while making the sauce.

3 Heat the crème fraîche and pesto together in the pasta saucepan. Return the pasta and roasted vegetables to the pan, and toss together, adding some of the Parmesan.

4 Serve immediately in a heated dish, sprinkled with the remaining Parmesan.

cook now, eat later

TO PREPARE AND COOK AHEAD The roast vegetables can be roasted well ahead of time, or even the day before, and reheated in a hot oven as you boil the pasta. If liked, the pasta can be cooked, drained, refreshed and covered up to 6 hours in advance. As can the broccoli and asparagus: boil in salted water for 3 minutes then plunge into cold water and drain.

TO FREEZE Not suitable.

TO COOK IN THE AGA Roast the onions and red peppers on the floor of the Roasting Oven for 30 minutes, turning from time to time, until just done. Add the courgettes after 15 minutes. Cook all else on the Boiling Plate.

Chilli-hot monkfish pasta with vegetables

Billingsgate Market now has a brilliant training school for young fishmongers. This is an adaptation of a recipe the chef made us. Buy young mangetout and tiny fine beans.

Serves 6

700g (1½ lb) monkfish, skinned and cut into 2cm (¾ in) pieces	1 onion, finely chopped
5 tablespoons chilli dipping sauce	2 garlic cloves, crushed
350g (12 oz) dried pasta shells	200ml (7 fl oz) white wine
400g (14 oz) fine French beans, cut into 3	4 tablespoons hoisin sauce
350g (12 oz) mangetout, cut diagonally	6 tablespoons crème fraîche
1–2 tablespoons olive oil	salt and freshly ground black pepper

1 Turn the monkfish over in the chilli dipping sauce.

2 Cook the pasta in boiling, generously salted water until just cooked al dente. Refresh in plenty of running cold water.

3 Blanch the beans for 3 minutes in boiling salted water, add the mangetout and continue to blanch for another 30 seconds. Drain and refresh in cold water.

4 Heat the oil in a large pan and sauté the onion and garlic without colouring until soft. Add the wine and reduce to 3 tablespoons. Toss in the monkfish, stir for 1 minute then add the pasta and vegetables. Heat for a few minutes, stirring continually, then add the hoisin sauce and the crème fraîche to the pasta. Season and serve immediately while everything is piping hot.

cook now, eat later

TO PREPARE AND COOK AHEAD Marinate the monkfish in the chilli dipping sauce for up to 8 hours ahead, keeping it in the fridge. Cook the pasta, drain, refresh in cold water, drain again and cover with clingfilm. Blanch the beans and mangetout as directed, drain, refresh and drain again. Cook the pasta and vegetables up to 6 hours ahead, and reheat in boiling water at the last minute.

TO FREEZE Not suitable.

TO COOK IN THE AGA Cook the pasta and blanch the beans and mangetout on the Boiling Plate. Sauté the onion and garlic on the Boiling Plate, and then transfer to the Simmering Oven until soft, about 10–15 minutes. Continue step 4 on the Boiling Plate as directed.

Penne pasta with Parma ham

A wonderful pasta recipe. Serve with chunks of fresh bread and fresh green salad leaves if liked. The dry-cured ham comes usually in packets of between 70g and 100g. Asparagus tips are the short thin asparagus spears sold in supermarkets but not usually available in greengrocers.

Serves 6

500g (1 lb 2 oz) dried penne pasta
salt and freshly ground black pepper
225g (8 oz) asparagus tips
2 × 70g (2½ oz) Serrano, Parma or Black Forest ham, snipped into pieces

450g (1 lb) small chestnut mushrooms, sliced
1 × 400ml carton crème fraîche
about 50g (2 oz) Parmesan, freshly grated
a good handful of chopped fresh parsley

1 Cook the pasta in a large pan of boiling salted water over a high heat, as directed on the packet, until al dente. Some 3 minutes before the end of cooking, add the asparagus tips. Drain and refresh in cold water, then set aside to drain.

2 Fry the ham in a large non-stick frying pan until crisp. Remove half of the ham and keep warm.

3 Add the mushrooms to the pan and stir with the ham for a moment, then mix in the crème fraîche and half the Parmesan. Season with a little salt and pepper (go easy on the salt as the ham is salty), and bring to the boil.

4 Return the cooked pasta and asparagus to the first large pan, and add the contents of the frying pan (ham and crème fraîche). Stir well until piping hot, and check the seasoning.

5 Sprinkle over the remaining Parmesan, reserved ham and the parsley. Serve at once.

cook now, eat later

TO PREPARE AND COOK AHEAD Cook the pasta up to 6 hours ahead, adding the asparagus for the last 3 minutes. Drain the pasta, leave in the colander, refresh in cold water, drain again and cover with clingfilm. Fry the ham until crisp and leave in the pan. About 5 minutes before serving, re-crisp the ham for a moment, remove half and keep warm. Continue as from step 3.

TO FREEZE Not suitable.

TO COOK IN THE AGA Cook the pasta and ham on the Boiling Plate. Keep half of the ham warm in the Simmering Oven. Finish on the Boiling Plate.

Pistou pasta with rocket ^V

A very simple recipe, which will take just 15 minutes to make from scratch – but you can prepare ahead as well. Serve with a green leaf salad.

Serves 6

350g (12 oz) dried penne pasta
150ml (¼ pint) white wine
2 shallots, finely chopped
450g (1 lb) mixed varieties of wild
    mushrooms, coarsely sliced
salt and freshly ground black pepper
4 tablespoons pouring double cream
1 × 50g (2 oz) bag rocket, removing
    some of the end stalks to add to the
    pistou

coarsely grated Parmesan to serve

PISTOU

a very good handful of fresh basil
    (leaves and stalks)
1 fat garlic clove, peeled
rocket stalks (see above)
about 4 tablespoons olive oil

1 First boil a pan of salted water for the pasta. When boiling, add the pasta and cook for about 12 minutes or according to packet instructions.

2 Then make the pistou. Measure the basil, garlic and rocket stalks into a food processor and quickly process. Then add the olive oil and process again. The oil doesn't mix well, but it takes on the flavour of the garlic and herbs.

3 Boil the wine in a large frying pan with the shallots and reduce for a few minutes. Add all of the mushrooms and stir over a high heat for a few minutes until the mushrooms are cooked and the liquid has reduced to 2 tablespoons. Season with salt and pepper. Add the cream and pistou, stirring to mix.

4 Drain the pasta and add to the mushroom mixture in the pan. Check the seasoning.

5 At the last moment stir in the rocket leaves, then serve with the Parmesan.

cook now, eat later

TO PREPARE AND COOK AHEAD Chop the shallots and slice the mushrooms up to 8 hours ahead. Make the pistou, cover and keep in the fridge for up to 24 hours. You could cook, drain, refresh, cover and chill the pasta up to 6 hours ahead.

TO FREEZE Not suitable.

TO COOK IN THE AGA Use the Boiling Plate to cook the mushrooms and the pasta.

Salmon coulibiac

Make the rice and salmon mixture some time ahead if it suits you. Leave covered in the fridge overnight then assemble the coulibiac on the day it is being eaten.

Serves 6

175g (6 oz) Uncle Ben's rice and
   wild rice
300ml (½ pint) water
1 teaspoon salt
50g (2 oz) butter
1 large Spanish onion, chopped
175g (6 oz) button mushrooms,
   quartered
salt and freshly ground black pepper

450g (1 lb) salmon fillet, skinned
2 good tablespoons chopped
   fresh parsley

TO ASSEMBLE
1 × 270g packet filo pastry, about
   6 sheets
about 50g (2 oz) butter, melted

Lightly grease a baking tray. Preheat the oven to 200°C/400°F/Gas 6.

1 First cook the rice. Measure it into a pan and add the water and salt. Bring to the boil, cover and simmer gently for about 15 minutes until the rice is tender and the liquid has been absorbed.

2 Melt the butter in a medium pan, add the onion and cook gently for about 10 minutes, until the onion is soft. Add the mushrooms to the pan and toss over a high heat for a few moments. Season with salt and pepper.

3 Cut the salmon into two pieces if necessary so that it will fit into the pan in a single layer. Add the salmon to the onion and mushrooms, cover and simmer gently for about 10 minutes until the salmon is cooked. Flake the fish into fairly large pieces – this can be done still in the pan. Add to the rice and stir in the parsley. Mix well, adjust seasoning and allow to cool.

4 Place 3 sheets of filo, slightly overlapping, side by side (about 30.5 × 38cm/12 × 15 in) on a baking sheet. Brush with most of the melted butter. Lay 3 more sheets on top. Spoon the filling down the centre of the filo (leaving large gaps at the side). Fold the pastry over the top and crimp the edges at the join. Squeeze the parcel so that it is long and thin and quite pointed at the top. Brush with a little more melted butter before cooking.

5 Bake in the preheated oven for about 40 minutes until the filo is golden and crisp and the filling hot throughout. Serve with *Lighter Herb Sauce* (see page 39) or low-fat crème fraîche and a green salad.

TO PREPARE AND COOK AHEAD Prepare the rice and salmon mixture up to 24 hours before, cool quickly and keep covered in the fridge. Assemble the coulibiac the day it is being eaten, up to 12 hours ahead.

TO FREEZE Not suitable.

TO COOK IN THE AGA Bring the rice to the boil in 250ml (9 fl oz) water on the Boiling Plate, cover and put into the Simmering Oven for about 15 minutes until tender. Cook the onion, covered, in the Simmering Oven for about 15–20 minutes until tender. Add the mushrooms and the salmon, and return to the Simmering Oven, covered, until the fish flakes and is opaque. Bake the assembled coulibiac on a baking sheet on the floor of the Roasting Oven until golden, about 20–25 minutes. You may need to slide the cold sheet in on the second set of runners if it's getting too brown.

Phad Thai noodles with seafood

A healthy fresh recipe, inspired by my much admired friend Ken Hom, the king of Chinese and Eastern cooking.

Serves 6

175g (6 oz) Thai rice noodles or fine egg noodles	100g (4 oz) baby sweetcorn, cut into 4 lengthways
150g (5 oz) sugar-snap peas, cut thinly on the diagonal	100g (4 oz) beansprouts
2 tablespoons sunflower oil	375g (12 oz) mixed seafood (i.e. fresh prawns, scallops, squid)
1 garlic clove, crushed	2 tablespoons sherry
1 x 2.5cm (1 in) piece fresh root ginger, finely grated	4 tablespoons soy sauce
2 red chillies, seeded and finely chopped	2 tablespoons oyster sauce
150g (5 oz) shiitake mushrooms, sliced	2 tablespoons lime juice
1 leek, sliced lengthways into thin batons	a few salted peanuts (optional) and sliced spring onions to garnish

1 Cook the noodles according to the packet instructions. For the last minute add the sugar-snap peas to the noodle pan. Drain and refresh lightly.

2 Heat the oil in a large frying pan or wok over a high heat until very hot. Add the garlic, ginger and chillies and fry for 2–3 minutes. Add the mushrooms, leek, baby corn and beansprouts and stir-fry for about 5 minutes.

3 When the vegetables are nearly cooked, add the seafood to the pan with the sherry, soy and oyster sauces and lime juice.

4 When the seafood is cooked through, stir in the noodles and sugar-snap peas, and mix well over a low heat for a few minutes.

5 Turn into a serving dish, and garnish with peanuts, if using, and spring onions.

cook now, eat later

TO PREPARE AHEAD Chop all the vegetables, cover and keep in the fridge until needed, up to 8 hours ahead. Stir-fry just before serving.

TO FREEZE Not suitable.

TO COOK IN THE AGA Boil the noodles and stir-fry the vegetables on the Boiling Plate.

Spicy turkey fajitas

If using cooked turkey or chicken, marinate for half an hour and add to the spring onions and red pepper.

Serves 6 (2 per person)

about 700g (1½ lb) raw turkey or chicken breast, cut into thin strips

juice of 2 limes

a dash of Tabasco sauce

2 tablespoons olive oil, plus a little extra

8 spring onions, finely sliced on the diagonal

salt and freshly ground black pepper

12 wheat fajitas or tortillas

1 large red pepper, thinly sliced

¾ teaspoon each of ground coriander, turmeric and paprika

TO SERVE

soured cream or crème fraîche, romaine or cos lettuce, mango chutney

Preheat the oven to 160°C/325°F/Gas 3.

1 Marinate the turkey or chicken in a bowl with the lime juice, Tabasco, measured olive oil, spring onions and salt and pepper. Leave for 30 minutes, or more if time allows.

2 Wrap the 12 fajitas or tortillas in foil and put into the oven for about 5 minutes to warm.

3 Lift the turkey or chicken and spring onions from the marinade using a slotted spoon. Heat a little olive oil in a frying pan and fry the meat in batches with the spring onions and red pepper until golden brown and cooked through. Return all of the meat to the pan, add the spices and cook for a further few minutes. Pour over any remaining marinade from the bowl and cook for 1 further minute.

4 Put the soured cream or crème fraîche, lettuce and mango chutney in 3 separate bowls. Transfer the warm fajitas to a basket, and spoon the meat into a serving dish.

5 Spread each quarter of a fajita with mango chutney, soured cream, then add lettuce and some of the spicy turkey and vegetable. Roll up and slice in half on the diagonal.

cook now, eat later

TO PREPARE AHEAD Marinate the turkey or chicken up to 24 hours ahead.

TO FREEZE Not suitable.

TO COOK IN THE AGA Warm the fajitas on a plate tightly covered with clingfilm. Put into the Simmering Oven for no more than 30 minutes (or in a 4-oven Aga Warming Oven for up to 1 hour). Stir-fry the ingredients on the Boiling Plate.

Turkey salad with
avocado, bacon and pesto dressing

Another tasty way to use up the fresh leftover turkey at Christmas, or a lovely summer buffet dish if made with chicken.

Serves 6

175g (6 oz) bacon, cut into small pieces
450g (1 lb) cooked turkey or chicken,
   free from skin and bone
salt and freshly ground black pepper
50g (2 oz) black olives in olive oil, stoned
   and cut in half
2 just ripe avocados
3 heaped tablespoons chopped
   fresh parsley
a small bag of mixed salad leaves

DRESSING
6 tablespoons olive oil
3 tablespoons balsamic vinegar
1 tablespoon caster sugar
2 tablespoons pesto

1 Measure the dressing ingredients into a jug and mix together. Season with salt and pepper.

2 Fry the bacon pieces until crisp, and keep warm.

3 Cut the turkey or chicken into neat pieces, season and toss in two-thirds of the dressing with the olives. This can be left to marinate overnight if you have time.

4 Peel the avocados, remove the stones, and cut the flesh into large pieces. Gently coat with the remaining dressing and season well.

5 Just before serving, mix together the turkey or chicken, avocado, parsley and salad leaves. Pile on to a pretty serving dish, and sprinkle over the hot bacon.

cook now, eat later

TO PREPARE AHEAD Prepare up to the end of step 3. Cover and keep in the fridge up to 24 hours ahead.

TO FREEZE Not suitable.

TO COOK IN THE AGA Fry the bacon on the Boiling Plate the day before and warm in the Simmering Oven for 5 minutes when needed.

Piquant chicken with basil

A delicious family chicken recipe, which will be popular with all ages. Once you've bought the chicken breasts the rest of the ingredients are more than likely to be in the store-cupboard.

Serves 6

2 tablespoons sunflower oil	1 tablespoon dry mustard powder
a good knob of butter	3 tablespoons light muscovado sugar
6 chicken breasts, skin removed	3–4 tablespoons tomato ketchup
salt and freshly ground black pepper	3 tablespoons soy sauce
1 small onion, finely chopped	1–2 tablespoons tomato paste
2 fat garlic cloves, crushed	1 × 400g can chopped tomatoes
2 tablespoons cider or wine vinegar	6 sprigs of fresh basil, shredded

Preheat the oven to 190°C/375°F/Gas 5.

1 Measure the oil and butter into a large non-stick frying pan and brown the chicken in two batches for 4–5 minutes on each side. Put in a shallow ovenproof dish and season.

2 Lower the heat and add the onion and garlic to the pan. Cover and cook gently until the onion is tender, stirring occasionally, about 10 minutes. Add the remaining ingredients, except the basil, to the pan, season and pour over the chicken.

3 Cook in the preheated oven for about 20 minutes, until the chicken is tender. To test that the chicken is cooked cut into a breast with a sharp knife: the juices from the chicken should be clear.

4 Scatter with the fresh basil and serve with pasta and a mixed green salad.

cook now, eat later

TO PREPARE AND COOK AHEAD Cook completely ahead, to the end of step 3, cool quickly, cover and refrigerate for up to 24 hours. To serve, cover and reheat in the oven preheated to 190°C/375°F/Gas 5 for about 30–40 minutes until piping hot. Scatter with the basil to serve.

TO FREEZE Cool, pack and freeze the cooked chicken without the basil. Freeze for up to 3 months. Thaw for about 6 hours at room temperature or overnight in the fridge. Reheat to serve as above.

TO COOK IN THE AGA Cook on the grid shelf on the floor of the Roasting Oven for about 20 minutes, depending on the size of the chicken breasts.

Aromatic Thai rice ^V

This is delicious, and good with many oriental meat and fish dishes. Use any par-boiled rice (easy-cook rice), i.e. a supermarket brand such as Uncle Ben's, with which I find it far easier to get light separate grains than with white Thai rice. Use a good chicken stock if you are not vegetarian.

Serves 4–6

3 tablespoons sunflower oil	1 lemongrass bulb, crushed lightly with a
1 medium onion, chopped	rolling pin
1 red chilli, seeded and finely chopped	1 good teaspoon salt
1 fat garlic clove, crushed	500ml (18 fl oz) vegetable stock
1 teaspoon garam masala	½ lime (in a whole piece)
350g (12 oz) par-boiled rice	

1 Heat the oil in a heavy-based pan, add the onion and cook for a few minutes until starting to soften.

2 Add the chilli, garlic, garam masala, rice, lemongrass and salt, and stir.

3 Pour in the stock and add the half lime. Bring to the boil, stir, cover and simmer very gently for about 10 minutes, or until all the liquid has been absorbed. Remove the lemongrass and lime, having squeezed out any juice.

cook now, eat later

TO PREPARE AND COOK AHEAD Cook the rice then turn into a bowl, cool rapidly and keep in the fridge for up to 6 hours. To reheat, place the rice on a large sheet of buttered foil and sprinkle with a little water. Wrap in a neat, tightly sealed parcel and bake in the oven preheated to 150°C/300°F/Gas 2 for about 25–30 minutes until piping hot.

TO FREEZE Not suitable.

TO COOK IN THE AGA Bring the rice to the boil on the boiling plate, stir, cover and transfer to the Simmering Oven for about 15–20 minutes or until all the liquid has been absorbed.

Thai pork curry

Traditionally Thai dishes do not contain flour, but I think it gives the sauce a more stable consistency. If you prefer, use chicken, a small breast each, or prawns.

Serves 6

700g (1½ lb) pork fillet, cut into fine strips	2 tablespoons Thai fish sauce
2–3 tablespoons red Thai curry paste	1 tablespoon granulated sugar
2 tablespoons sunflower oil	1 × 220g can water chestnuts, drained and halved
2 large onions, thinly sliced	juice and finely grated zest of ½ lime
1 level tablespoon plain flour	chopped fresh parsley or coriander
1 × 400ml can coconut milk	salt and freshly ground black pepper

1 Marinate the pork in 1 tablespoon of the curry paste for 30 minutes.

2 Heat the oil in a large frying pan, add the onions and cook gently for about 10 minutes until they are tender. Lift the onions out on to a plate.

3 Increase the heat and brown the pork. This will probably have to be done in 2 batches. Remove the pork from the pan and return the onions with 1–2 tablespoons red Thai curry paste and the flour. Stirring well, add the coconut milk, fish sauce, sugar, water chestnuts and pork. Bring to the boil, cover and cook gently for about 5 minutes, until the pork and sauce are just boiling.

4 Just before serving add the lime juice and zest and lots of parsley or coriander. Taste for seasoning. Serve with rice.

cook now, eat later

TO PREPARE AND COOK AHEAD Complete to the end of step 3. Cool quickly, cover and keep in the fridge for up to 24 hours. Reheat until piping hot, adding the lime and parsley or coriander to serve.

TO FREEZE Cool quickly and freeze at the end of step 3, omitting the water chestnuts. Thaw overnight in the fridge, add the water chestnuts and reheat until piping hot. Expect the sauce to separate on thawing. It will come together once reheated in a pan, stirring.

TO COOK IN THE AGA Cook the onions, covered, in the Simmering Oven for about 20–30 minutes until tender. Brown the pork on the Boiling Plate, then continue as in stages 3 and 4.

Baked sausages with double onion marmalade

This method of cooking sausages keeps them wonderfully succulent.

Serves 6

about 1 tablespoon sunflower oil	225ml (8 fl oz) red wine
about 25g (1 oz) butter	50ml (2 fl oz) red or white wine vinegar
900g (2 lb) good-quality sausages	2 tablespoons caster sugar
450g (1 lb) red onions, thinly sliced	salt and freshly ground black pepper
2 large white onions, about 450g (1 lb)	about 3 tablespoons chopped
in weight, thinly sliced	fresh parsley

Preheat the oven to 200°C/400°F/Gas 6.

1 Heat the oil and butter over a high heat in a large frying pan and brown the sausages evenly. You will need to do this in 2 batches. Lift the sausages out and drain on kitchen paper.

2 Pour off excess fat so that there is about 2 tablespoons left in the pan. Add the onions to the pan and cook gently, stirring occasionally, for 10–15 minutes or until soft.

3 Add the wine, vinegar, sugar and seasoning to the onions. Bring to the boil and allow to bubble for a couple of minutes. Transfer to an ovenproof dish.

4 Arrange the sausages in a single layer on top of the onions and cook, uncovered, in the preheated oven for about 45 minutes. Stir the onions occasionally: they should be soft.

5 Scatter with lots of parsley and serve with mashed potato (see page 106).

cook now, eat later

TO PREPARE AND COOK AHEAD Cook to the end of step 4. Cool, cover and store in the fridge for up to 2 days. To reheat, cover and cook in the oven preheated to 190°C/375°F/Gas 5 for about 30–40 minutes or until piping hot. Scatter with parsley to serve.

TO FREEZE Cook to the end of stage 4. Cool, pack into a freezer container and freeze for up to 3 months. Thaw overnight in the fridge. Reheat as above.

TO COOK IN THE AGA Brown the sausages on the floor of the Roasting Oven in a pan lined with non-stick paper, turning them occasionally. Cook the onions, covered, in the Simmering Oven for about 30 minutes. Transfer the onions and sausages to an ovenproof dish, and put on the grid shelf on the floor of the Roasting Oven for about 45 minutes.

HOT PUDDINGS

Few people these days think of serving a hot pudding, and excuses range from 'it takes too much time' and 'it's complicated' to 'it's fattening' . . . But the truth is that none of these is strictly true. Sweet things are generally considered to be more calorific, but most of the puddings here are based on fruit, a healthy touch at the end of a meal. And if you really are worried about your weight, simply have a smaller helping and say no to the accompanying cream (that's where most calories lie).

Neither is it true that hot puddings are more complicated to cook. Something like the tart on page 152 is simplicity itself, and I bet your guests won't recognise that the tart base is slices of brioche! And a novice cook could quickly master something like the caramelised peaches. And of course preparing stages of a dish ahead makes it all so much easier when pulling everything together at the last minute.

But the best news about these hot puddings is that they are so quick to make. All can be prepared well in advance, and then baked just before serving, none of them taking longer than 40 minutes (some can even be baked ahead and reheated). What could be easier than putting your hot pudding into the oven as you finish serving the main course? And most of the puddings here even save you time on the washing-up: they are served from the dish in which they were cooked.

Serve hot puddings with a cold pouring cream such as single. If you want a dollop of cream, use low-fat crème fraîche rather than double cream (not so rich). And remember that if you heat crème fraîche or soured cream, they become the consistency of milk – not what you want for this purpose. Always serve them cold.

Toffee Apple Puddings with Toffee Sauce **V**

Pear Tarte Tatin **V**

Cherry Queen of Puddings **V**

Apricot Brioche Tart **V**

Easy Lime and Lemon Meringue Pie **V**

Apple, Lemon and Cinnamon Strudel **V**

Saucy Chocolate and Walnut Pudding **V**

Caramelised Peaches with Brandy **V**

For more pudding ideas, see:

Cold Desserts (see pages 162–181)

Mincemeat Bread and Butter Pudding (see page 230)

Apple Mincemeat Alaska (see page 239)

Toffee apple puddings with toffee sauce V

Deliciously naughty puddings, which are very quick and easy, and can be made in moulds (available from good kitchen shops and by mail order), and baked later. There may be too much toffee sauce for you, but it keeps in the fridge for 1 month and is excellent over ice-cream.

Serves 8

100g (4 oz) butter or baking margarine,
    at room temperature
50g (2 oz) light muscovado sugar
1 tablespoon golden syrup
2 eggs
150g (5 oz) self-raising flour
1 level teaspoon baking powder

TOPPING
200g (7 oz) butter
200g (7 oz) light muscovado sugar
juice of ½ lemon
2–3 dessert apples, peeled, cored and
    chopped into sultana-sized pieces

TOFFEE SAUCE
50g (2 oz) butter
150g (5 oz) light muscovado sugar
150g (5 oz) golden syrup
1 × 170g can evaporated milk
juice of ½ lemon (optional)

Lightly grease the insides of eight 150ml (¼ pint) pudding moulds. Preheat the oven to 220°C/425°F/Gas 7.

1 First make the topping. Melt the butter and sugar together in a small pan over a gentle heat, add the lemon juice and apples, and divide between the pudding moulds.

2 Measure the cake ingredients into a food processor and mix until blended, scraping down the sides of the bowl once. (Be careful not to over-beat.) Or mix the ingredients in a bowl with an electric hand-held whisk. Spoon the mixture on to the apples in the pudding moulds: two-thirds fill each one. Cover each mould with a square of buttered foil.

3 Line a small roasting tin (the right size to fit the 8 pudding moulds comfortably) with a piece of kitchen paper, put in the moulds and half fill the tin with boiling water. Cover completely with foil and bake in the preheated oven for 30–35 minutes until the puddings are well risen and firm to the touch.

4 Meanwhile, make the sauce. Measure the butter, sugar and syrup into a pan, and heat gently until melted and liquid. Gently boil for 5 minutes. Remove from the heat and gradually add the evaporated milk. The sauce is now ready. Leave on one side and heat to piping hot to serve. If you find the sauce too sweet, add lemon juice to taste.

5 When the puddings are ready, remove from the oven, loosen the sides, and turn out. Serve drizzled with hot toffee sauce.

cook now, eat later

TO PREPARE AND COOK AHEAD Prepare to the end of step 2 up to 24 hours ahead. Keep the unbaked puds chilled until ready to bake, but they will take a little longer to cook from cold. The puddings can also be baked and then kept warm, still in the moulds, in a low oven at 140°C/275°F/Gas 1 for up to 40 minutes, still covered with foil.

TO FREEZE Not suitable.

TO COOK IN THE AGA At step 3, slide the roasting tin, half filled with hot water and covered with foil, directly on to the floor of the Roasting Oven for about 15 minutes. Turn round once and continue to bake for a further 15 minutes until well risen and firm to the touch. Keep warm in the moulds for up to 40 minutes in the roasting tin in the Simmering Oven, still covered with foil.

TIP 'Bain-marie' is the French name for cooking in a roasting tin of boiling water to come half-way up the dish, making the cooking even but not too fast. If cooking in ramekins, line the base of the roasting tin with a piece of kitchen paper and sit the ramekins on top. This stops them sliding about. If using an aluminium tin, put a wedge of lemon in the water, as this will prevent a black line appearing.

Pear tarte tatin ^V

You can of course use apples instead. Use any leftover pastry for cheese straws (see page 249). Do not use a loose-bottomed tin as the liquid will run out of the bottom!

Serves 6

100g (4 oz) butter	900g–1.1kg (2–2½ lb) pears, ripe but firm
100g (4 oz) muscovado sugar	1 × 500g packet puff pastry

Line a 20cm (8 in) round shallow cake tin, 3cm (1½ in) deep, with a circle of non-stick baking paper. Preheat the oven to 220°C/425°F/Gas 7.

1 Gently heat the butter and sugar together in a small pan until both have melted and the mixture is smooth and a golden straw colour. Pour into the prepared cake tin and spread out evenly with the back of a wet spoon to cover the base of the tin. You may not need to do this: it may just run over the base by itself.

2 Peel, core and slice the pears, about 5mm (¼ in) thick. Arrange in overlapping circles on top of the mixture to use all of the pears. They will come right to the top of the tin.

3 Roll out the pastry on a lightly floured work surface so that it is just larger than the diameter of the cake tin. Place the pastry over the pears and trim off the excess. Push the pastry edges down into the tin to neaten.

4 Bake in the preheated oven for about 20 minutes until the pastry is a good golden brown. Allow to cool for about 10 minutes. Leaving the tart in the tin, carefully tip the tin to drain off the juice. Boil up the juices in a small pan until a pouring consistency.

5 Carefully invert the tart on to a heatproof serving plate. Pour the thickened juices over the tart and dust with icing sugar. Serve warm or hot with Greek yogurt or crème fraîche.

cook now, eat later

TO PREPARE AND COOK AHEAD Step 1 can be completed up to 2 days ahead. Up to 8 hours ahead the tart can be completely made. Drain off the juices whilst hot and boil to thicken just before serving. Reheat the tart in a hot oven at 200°C/400°F/Gas 6 for 15 minutes. Cover if getting too brown. Turn out, and pour the thickened sauce over it.

TO FREEZE Not suitable.

TO COOK IN THE AGA Cook the assembled tart on the grid shelf on the floor of the Roasting Oven for about 20 minutes. Slide the cold sheet on to the second set of runners after 10 minutes if getting too brown.

Cherry queen of puddings ^V

If preferred, use raspberry jam, but I think cherry is best. You could also use mincemeat at Christmas.

Serves 6

600ml (1 pint) milk	3 eggs, separated
25g (1 oz) butter	75g (3 oz) fresh fine white breadcrumbs
finely grated zest of 1 lemon	4 good tablespoons cherry jam, warmed
225g (8 oz) caster sugar	

Preheat the oven to 150°C/300°F/Gas 2 and grease a 1.4 litre (2½ pint) shallow (about 5cm/2 in) ovenproof dish, one that will fit flat in a roasting tin.

1 To start the custard base, very gently warm the milk in a small saucepan. Add the butter, lemon zest and 50g (2 oz) of the sugar, and stir until dissolved.

2 Lightly whisk the egg yolks in a bowl and gradually pour in and whisk in the warmed milk. Sprinkle the breadcrumbs over the base of the buttered dish and pour in the custard. Leave to stand for about 15 minutes for the breadcrumbs to absorb the liquid.

3 Carefully transfer the dish to a roasting tin and fill the tin half-way with boiling water. Bake in the preheated oven for about 25–30 minutes until the custard has set.

4 Whisk the egg whites on maximum speed in an electric mixer. When stiff, add the remaining sugar 1 teaspoon at a time (whisking on maximum speed) until stiff and shiny.

5 Remove the custard from the oven and pour over the jam. Spread the meringue on top. Arrange the top in rough peaks. Return to the oven and bake for about 35–40 minutes until the meringue is pale golden all over and crisp. Serve at once with cream.

cook now, eat later

TO PREPARE AND COOK AHEAD Bake the custard base, and spread with the cherry jam up to 24 hours ahead. Keep in the fridge. Then whisk and bake the meringue, see stages 4 and 5 (the cooking time may be a little longer).

TO FREEZE Not suitable.

TO COOK IN THE AGA Bake the custard (step 3) on the grid shelf on the floor of the Roasting Oven with the cold shelf on the second set of runners for about 20 minutes. Transfer to the Simmering Oven for about 15 minutes or until set. At step 5, return to the Roasting Oven on the grid shelf on the floor with the cold shelf on the second set of runners, for about 8 minutes, turning around after 4 minutes until lightly golden brown, then transfer to the Simmering Oven for about 10 minutes until crisp.

Apricot brioche tart $^\vee$

A wonderfully quick and easy tart, which is good made with canned pears as well. If I was giving a numerical rating to this recipe, I would give 10 out of 10!

Serves 6–8

1 egg	2 × 400g (14 oz) cans apricot halves,
2 tablespoons caster sugar	drained
1 × 250g tub mascarpone cheese	about 4 tablespoons demerara sugar
about 225g (8 oz) brioche, sliced about	icing sugar for dusting
1cm (½ in) thick from a loaf	

Lightly grease an ovenproof, shallow-sided dish, about 28cm (11 in) in diameter. Preheat the oven to 180°C/350°F/Gas 4.

1 Lightly whisk the egg and caster sugar together in a bowl. Add the mascarpone and whisk again until smooth and there are no lumps.

2 Arrange the brioche slices as neatly as possible in a single layer on the greased dish to completely cover it. Trim the brioche slices as necessary to fit. Spread the mascarpone mixture over the brioche slices to about 1cm (½ in) away from the edge. (You don't have to be accurate about this!)

3 Arrange the apricot halves neatly in circles over the mascarpone right to the edge of the brioche. Sprinkle the demerara sugar over the apricots.

4 Bake in the preheated oven for about 30–35 minutes until the custard is set and golden. Serve immediately with crème fraîche, and dust with icing sugar.

cook now, eat later

TO PREPARE AND COOK AHEAD Step 1 can be made and kept in the fridge up to 12 hours before. The brioche can be arranged in the dish, covered tightly for up to 12 hours ahead. The apricots can be drained. Assemble up to 2 hours before serving. Or bake the day before and reheat in the oven preheated to 190°C/375°F/Gas 5 for about 10 minutes. (It is best cooked just before serving, though.)

TO FREEZE Not suitable.

TO COOK IN THE AGA Bake on the floor of the Roasting Oven for about 8 minutes then slide on to the top set of runners in the Roasting Oven for a further 12 minutes until the custard is set and golden.

Easy lime and lemon meringue pie ^V

This delicious recipe is a bit of a cheat, as we are not making a classic lemon curd. Instead, we're using condensed milk. The base is a crumb crust without sugar as the filling is on the sweet side. Once made and baked, it is best eaten on the same day.

Serves 6

BASE	TOPPING
75g (3 oz) butter	3 egg whites
175g (6 oz) digestive biscuits, crushed	175g (6 oz) caster sugar

FILLING
1 × 394g can sweetened condensed milk
3 egg yolks
finely grated zest and juice of 2 limes and
    2 large lemons

You will need a 23cm (9 in) fluted china flan dish, or shallow, straight-sided round dish about 4cm (1½ in) deep. Preheat the oven to 190°C/375°F/Gas 5.

1 For the base, melt the butter in a medium-sized pan. Remove the pan from the heat and stir in the biscuit crumbs. Press the mixture into the flan dish using the back of a spoon to bring the crumbs up round the edge of the dish, and smooth the base evenly.

2 For the filling, pour the condensed milk into a bowl, then beat in the egg yolks, lemon and lime zest and strained juices. The mixture will seem to thicken slightly on standing, then loosen again as soon as it is stirred. This is caused by the combination of condensed milk and citrus juices and is nothing to worry about. Pour the mixture into the biscuit-lined dish.

3 For the topping, measure the egg whites into a large, grease-free bowl and, preferably using an electric hand whisk (or otherwise a balloon whisk), whisk the egg whites until stiff but not dry. Now start adding the measured sugar slowly, 1 teaspoon at a time, whisking well between each addition at full speed. When about two-thirds of the sugar has been added, the process can be speeded up. In total it should take about 8 minutes (2–3 minutes with one of the latest free-standing mixers).

4 Pile separate spoons of meringue over the surface of the filling, then spread gently to cover the filling to the biscuit edge. Lightly swirl the meringue, then bake in the preheated oven for about 15–20 minutes or until the meringue is pale golden. The meringue should be soft inside and a little crisp on top. Leave aside for about 30 minutes before serving warm. This will give the filling time to firm up a little and therefore make serving easier.

cook now, eat later

TO PREPARE AND COOK AHEAD The flan dish can be lined with the biscuit crumb mix, covered and kept in the fridge for up to 3 days. The filling can be mixed, covered and kept in the fridge for up to 8 hours before baking. Once baked, the pie can be eaten warm or cold, but the meringue shrinks a little on standing.

TO FREEZE Not suitable.

TO COOK IN THE AGA Bake the assembled pie on the grid shelf of the Roasting Oven on the third set of runners for about 2–3 minutes until a pale brown colour, then transfer to the centre of the Simmering Oven for a further 15 minutes or so.

Apple, lemon and cinnamon strudel ⱽ

An apple strudel used to be such a popular recipe, and we think it's worth a comeback. It is so quick and easy to make too. The breadcrumbs help to absorb some of the liquid from the apples, and stop the pastry going soggy.

Serves 6

about 6 sheets filo pastry (if the pastry is very thin, use 9 sheets)

about 50g (2 oz) butter, melted

about 25g (1 oz) fresh breadcrumbs

FILLING

1 large cooking apple (about 400g/14 oz peeled weight), peeled, cored and sliced

finely grated zest and juice of ½ lemon

50g (2 oz) demerara sugar

1 teaspoon mixed spice

1 teaspoon ground cinnamon

50g (2 oz) sultanas

ICING

a little lemon juice

175g (6 oz) icing sugar, sieved

Lightly grease a baking tray. Preheat the oven to 190°C/375°F/Gas 5.

1 Mix all the filling ingredients together in a bowl.

2 Place 3 sheets of filo, long sides together, side by side on a board, slightly overlapping in the middle where they join. They should measure altogether about 45 × 31cm (18 × 12 in). Brush with melted butter. Repeat with another 1 or 2 layers, buttering in between the pastry, using the total of 6 or 9 sheets. Sprinkle the top sheets with the breadcrumbs.

3 Spoon the filling into a third of the rectangle at the bottom of one end of the pastry (across the join) about 5cm (2 in) away from the edge and side. Cut away about 2.5cm (1 in) of pastry at the sides, from the top of the filling upwards (this helps prevent too much pastry being folded together).

4 Turn the sides in over the filling and roll up from the filling end into a sausage shape. Carefully lift the strudel on to the baking tray and brush all over with melted butter.

5 Bake in the preheated oven for about 35–40 minutes until the pastry is golden and crisp.

6 Mix the lemon juice with the sieved icing sugar to blend together (do not make it too runny or it will slide off the strudel). Spread or drizzle in a zig-zag pattern over the top of the strudel. Serve immediately with a good vanilla ice-cream or crème fraîche.

recipe continued overleaf

cook now, eat later

TO PREPARE AHEAD Prepare the strudel to the end of step 4. Cover and leave in a cool place for up to 8 hours before baking as in step 5, and icing.

TO FREEZE This freezes well after cooking. Cool the un-iced strudel then wrap and freeze for up to 3 months. Defrost at room temperature and reheat covered in foil in a moderate oven at 180°C/350°F/Gas 4 for about 10–15 minutes. Then ice.

TO COOK IN THE AGA Carefully lift the strudel on to a greased baking tray or non-stick paper. Slide on to the floor of the Roasting Oven for about 8 minutes, or until the bottom of the pastry is brown. Transfer to the grid shelf on the floor of the Roasting Oven for a further 10–12 minutes until golden brown. If getting too brown, slide the cold sheet on to the second set of runners.

Saucy chocolate and walnut pudding ^V

This is a classic recipe but usually made with lemon. The sponge goes on the bottom and the sauce is poured over the top: when cooked the sponge has risen and the sauce is at the bottom. If you are not keen on walnuts, leave them out, or replace with chocolate chips.

Serves 6

50g (2 oz) butter, melted, plus extra for greasing	50g (2 oz) shelled walnuts or pecans, coarsely chopped
4 eggs	icing sugar for sprinkling
100g (4 oz) caster sugar	
½ teaspoon vanilla extract	SAUCE
100g (4 oz) self-raising flour	100g (4 oz) light muscovado sugar
50g (2 oz) cocoa powder	3 tablespoons cocoa powder
2 teaspoons baking powder	450ml (¾ pint) boiling water

Lightly butter an ovenproof dish 1.4 litre (2½ pint) in capacity and 7.5–9cm (3–3½ in) deep. Preheat the oven to 180°C/350°F/Gas 4.

1 Whisk together the eggs, caster sugar and vanilla extract until well blended. Pour the melted butter on to the eggs and then sieve in the flour, cocoa powder and baking powder. Mix thoroughly then stir in the walnuts or pecans. Pour the mixture into the buttered dish.

2 To make the sauce, sieve the muscovado sugar and cocoa powder into a medium bowl and gradually whisk in the boiling water. Cool slightly, then pour the sauce over the pudding mixture.

3 Bake in the preheated oven for about 30–40 minutes until the sauce has sunk to the bottom, and the sponge is well risen, springy to the touch and a dark chocolate brown.

4 Sprinkle with icing sugar and serve immediately with cream, crème fraîche, custard, ice-cream, or all four!

cook now, eat later

TO PREPARE AHEAD Make the sponge mixture and sauce up to 4 hours ahead, but keep separately, the sponge in its buttered dish, and the sauce in its bowl. Spoon the sauce over the sponge just before baking.

TO FREEZE Not suitable.

TO COOK IN THE AGA Slide the pudding dish on to the lowest set of runners in the Roasting Oven for about 10 minutes until dark brown. Slide the cold sheet on to the second set of runners for a further 10 minutes or so until the pudding is springy to touch, and a dark chocolate brown.

Caramelised peaches with brandy V

The peaches can also be left whole for this recipe, when they look particularly tempting and delicious.

Serves 6

6 fresh peaches or nectarines	ground cinnamon
soft butter	brandy
demerara sugar	crème fraîche to serve

Preheat the oven to 200°C/400°F/Gas 6.

1 Peel the peaches or nectarines by dipping into boiling water until the skin is easy to remove (as you would skin a tomato). Cut in half and remove the stones. Dry with kitchen paper, then rub the rounded side of each peach or nectarine with soft butter.

2 Pack the peaches or nectarines cut side down into a dish in which they fit tightly. Sprinkle with demerara sugar and cinnamon and pour about 6 tablespoons of brandy into the dish around them.

3 Bake in the preheated oven for about 30 minutes until tender.

4 Serve hot with cream or *Brandy Ice-cream* (see page 232).

cook now, eat later

TO PREPARE AND COOK AHEAD Cook up to 12 hours ahead of time, but only for 20 minutes. Cover and store in a cool place for up to 12 hours. Reheat in a hot oven at 200°C/400°F/Gas 6 for about 10–15 minutes. Sprinkle with a little more demerara sugar first.

TO FREEZE Not suitable.

TO COOK IN THE AGA Bake on the top set of runners in the Roasting Oven for about 15 minutes until the peaches or nectarines are tender.

COLD DESSERTS

Every single recipe in this chapter can be made in advance – at least the day before – and indeed the majority can be frozen. This is exactly why cold desserts are so popular, of course: once you have a tray of mousses or a bowl of fruit salad in the fridge, or an ice-cream in the freezer, you can forget completely about one course of your meal and concentrate on the others.

The ice-creams are delicious and unusual. They are made from a whipped meringue and whipped cream mixture, so the volume is there before they are frozen. This means that they do not need any re-whisking, either by hand or in a machine, so that too saves time and energy. Another job that needn't be done. However, the ice-creams do contain raw egg, so do be aware when serving to the very young, the elderly or to pregnant ladies. Most eggs nowadays are stamped with a lion which is proof that the hen has been injected against salmonella. But, as with most things, there is often no guarantee.

You can go to town serving cold desserts, and I love decorating the plates. My icing sugar sifter works well, especially over the chocolate terrine, and I always have a spray of berries or currants if the dessert is fruit based. A good tip when serving ice-cream is to scoop it out into balls in advance and place back in the freezer, covered with clingfilm. This saves time, but also makes the ultimate serving much easier. Just remember to remove from the freezer 10 or so minutes in advance so that they come to eating temperature and texture.

A final thought. If you are serving two cold desserts, make sure they are quite different: one rich, gooey and calorific, the other something like a fruit salad or a sorbet. People can choose what they like – one or the other, or indeed both!

Double Chocolate Terrine **V**

Walnut Praline Parfait **V**

Quite the Best Summer Pudding **V**

Hazelnut Meringue Roulade with Passion-lemon Coulis **V**

Homemade Lemon Curd **V**

Divine Lemon Pots **V**

White Chocolate Mousses **V**

Lavender Crème Caramel **V**

Lemon Balm Ice-cream **V**

Melon Sorbet **V**

Orange Curd Ice-cream with Passionfruit and Orange **V**

Five-fruit Salad **V**

For more dessert ideas, see:

Hot Puddings section (see page 146)

Home Baking Section (see page 204)

Mincemeat Bread and Butter Pudding (see page 230)

Brandy Ice-cream (see page 232)

Frangipane Mince Pies (see page 232)

Apple Mincemeat Alaska (see page 239)

Double chocolate terrine V

Serve in thinnish slices as it is very naughty! Make the terrine 1 day ahead so that it's really firm.

Serves 10–12

WHITE CHOCOLATE LAYER	DARK CHOCOLATE LAYERS
200g (7 oz) white chocolate (Lindt Excellence)	350g (12 oz) dark chocolate (Bournville)
200ml (7 fl oz) double cream	450ml (¾ pint) double cream
	2 egg yolks
	2 tablespoons brandy

Line a 900g (2lb) loaf tin with clingfilm.

1 For the white chocolate layer, break into a bowl with the double cream and carefully melt together over a pan of hot water. Don't let the chocolate become too hot or it will go grainy; it should be slightly hotter than lukewarm. Stir until smooth. Leave to cool.

2 For the dark chocolate layers, break into a food processor and process to a fine powder. Boil half of the cream and pour in. Process until smooth then add the egg yolks and brandy. Mix until blended. Whisk the remaining cream in a bowl to soft peaks and fold into the dark chocolate mixture in a bowl. Pour some of this mixture to reach one-third of the way up the lined tin then transfer to the freezer for about 1 hour, until set. When just set, pour in the white chocolate and freeze for about 2 hours until set.

3 Spoon the remaining dark chocolate on top of the white mixture, cover and put back into the freezer for about 6 hours until firm or simply leave in the fridge overnight to set.

4 To serve, you may want to freeze the terrine for about 30 minutes, which makes cutting easier. Remove the clingfilm. Serve in slices (it helps to cut the slices with a hot knife).

cook now, eat later

TO PREPARE AHEAD This can be made up to 2 days ahead. Make completely and turn out, leaving the clingfilm intact. Peel off and decorate before serving straight from the fridge.

TO FREEZE Once set, turn out, wrap in a second layer of clingfilm and freeze for up to 1 month. Thaw for about 6 hours.

TO 'COOK' IN THE AGA Melt the chocolates in separate bowls on a tea-towel at the back of the Aga several hours ahead.

Walnut praline parfait ᵛ

A very easy and delicious dessert, generously given to me by Vicky, a close neighbour. Just take it out of the freezer about 10 minutes before serving – what could be easier!

Serves 8

4 eggs, separated	PRALINE
100g (4 oz) caster sugar	100g (4 oz) caster sugar
300ml (½ pint) pouring double cream	6 tablespoons water
1 teaspoon vanilla extract	100g (4 oz) walnut pieces

You will need 8 ramekins.

1 To make the praline, dissolve the sugar and water in a small saucepan (not non-stick), stirring until all the sugar is dissolved. Turn up the heat, discard the spoon, and boil until a light caramel colour. Stir in the walnuts and pour on to non-stick paper for the praline to set. Once the praline is cold, chop up into small pieces (about the size of a sultana).

2 Whisk the egg whites in a mixer, or with an electric hand whisk on maximum speed until stiff. Gradually add the sugar 1 teaspoon at a time until well incorporated and the mixture is stiff and glossy. Fold in the egg yolks.

3 Whisk the cream with the vanilla extract until just thick. Fold into the egg mixture, along with most of the chopped praline (reserve a little for garnish).

4 Pour into 8 ramekins, cover with clingfilm and freeze for a minimum of 12 hours.

5 Remove the parfait from the freezer about 10 minutes before serving, and top with the reserved walnut praline.

cook now, eat later

TO PREPARE AHEAD AND FREEZE Prepare and freeze up to 1 month before. In which case, forget the reserved praline, and simply sprinkle with icing sugar and some fresh mint.

TO COOK IN THE AGA Dissolve the sugar for the praline on the Simmering Plate, discard the spoon, then transfer to the Boiling Plate, and boil until a light caramel colour.

Quite the best summer pudding ^V

This summer pudding is all fruit and very little bread. I make it fairly shallow in a straight-sided soufflé dish or glass dish. The shallowness means that even though there is much more fruit than bread, the pudding doesn't collapse when turned out. There will be fruit left so serve it with the pudding, which should be really well chilled.

Serves 8

350g (12 oz) blackberries

350g (12 oz) blackcurrants

350g (12 oz) redcurrants

1 small punnet, about 150g (5 oz) blueberries, if available

350g (12 oz) caster sugar

225g (8 oz) raspberries

8 slices thin sliced bread, crusts removed

pouring cream to serve

You will need a 1.1 litre (2 pint) soufflé dish or straight-sided dish, 15 × 8cm (6 × 3 in).

1 Measure all the fruits except the raspberries into a pan with a tablespoon of water. Add the sugar and bring to the boil, then gently simmer until the fruits are just tender. Cool a little, then add the raspberries.

2 Cut the bread to shapes to fit the base and sides of the dish to about 5cm (2 in) up the side. Dip the bread into the juice first then line the dish, putting the fruit-soaked side nearest the dish. Fill the dish just under half full with some of the fruit, then put a layer of bread over the fruit. Add more fruit on top and finally the last slices of bread, spooning a little of the juice over the bread at the top. You should have about 200ml (7 fl oz) of fruit left over to serve with the pudding. Put a small plate on top, press down lightly, then cover with clingfilm and refrigerate overnight.

3 Turn out into a shallow dish a little larger than the summer pudding so that the juices are caught. I serve it with extra reserved fruit and pouring cream.

cook now, eat later

TO PREPARE AND COOK AHEAD Make up to 2 days ahead and keep in the fridge.

TO FREEZE Cover and freeze at the end of step 2. Thaw overnight at room temperature. The pudding will be quite soft after freezing.

TO COOK IN THE AGA Bring the fruits to the boil on the Boiling Plate, cover and transfer to the Simmering Oven for about 15 minutes or until the fruits are just tender.

Hazelnut meringue roulade with passion-lemon coulis ^V

A meringue roulade with the wonderful addition of hazelnuts. The coulis is stunning! You can make lemon curd with the egg yolks left over from the meringue.

Makes 8–10 slices

5 egg whites	COULIS
275g (10 oz) caster sugar	6 tablespoons lemon curd
50g (2 oz) shelled hazelnuts, roughly chopped	2 passionfruit
300ml (½ pint) double cream, whipped	GARNISH
	8 Cape gooseberries

Preheat the oven to 200°C/400°F/Gas 6. Line a 33 × 23cm (13 × 9 in) Swiss roll tin with greased non-stick baking paper, securing the corners with metal paperclips.

1 Whisk the egg whites in an electric mixer on full speed until very stiff. Gradually add the sugar, 1 teaspoon at a time, and still at high speed, whisk well between each addition. Whisk until very, very stiff and all the sugar had been included. Mix in two-thirds of the hazelnuts.

2 Spread the meringue mixture into the prepared tin and sprinkle the remaining hazelnuts evenly over the top. Bake in the preheated oven for about 12 minutes or until just coloured pale golden. Lower the oven temperature to 160°C/325°F/Gas 3 and continue baking for a further 20 minutes until firm to the touch.

3 Remove the meringue from the oven and turn, hazelnut side down, on to a sheet of non-stick baking paper. Remove the paper and paperclips from the base of the cooked meringue and allow to cool for about 10 minutes.

4 When cooled, spread the whipped cream over the meringue. Start to roll from the long end, fairly tightly, until rolled up like a Swiss roll. Wrap in non-stick paper and chill before serving.

5 To make the coulis, mix the lemon curd with the scooped-out seeds and juice from the passionfruit.

6 Serve the coulis alongside a slice of roulade. Garnish with a Cape gooseberry on each plate.

recipe continued overleaf

cook now, eat later

Homemade lemon curd

A wonderful way of using up egg yolks, having made meringues.

Makes 3 small jars

100g (4 oz) butter	grated zest and juice 3 lemons
225g (8 oz) caster sugar	5 egg yolks or 3 beaten eggs

1 Measure butter and sugar into a bowl. Stand over a pan of simmering water and sir occasionally until butter has melted. Stir lemon zest and juice and egg yolks (or eggs) into butter mixture. Cook for about 25 minutes until curd thickens, stirring occasionally. Do not allow to get too hot.

2 Remove from heat and pour into warm, clean jars.

cook now, eat later

Divine lemon pots ^V

Probably the easiest dessert you will ever make – and so delicious too! It came my way from a dear friend Di. Four of us play tennis every Monday and so often swap recipes and ideas over coffee! It has become a firm favourite ever since. You don't need to add the raspberries, and the brandy can be left out too, but we prefer it with!

Serves 8

600ml (1 pint) pouring double cream	16 fresh raspberries
150g (5 oz) caster sugar	3 tablespoons brandy
finely grated zest and juice of 3 lemons	

You will need 8 small coffee cups, wine glasses or tiny ramekins.

1 Heat the cream, sugar and lemon zest in a wide-based pan over a low heat until at simmering point. Stir continuously for about 3 minutes.

2 Remove from the heat and allow to cool slightly (until lukewarm).

3 Mix the lemon juice and brandy with the cooled cream and sugar, and stir.

4 Pour the lemon cream into the cups. Transfer to the fridge to set for a minimum of 2 hours. Arrange 2 raspberries on top of each pot when the cream has set.

cook now, eat later

TO PREPARE AND COOK AHEAD These can be made up to 24 hours before serving, and kept in the fridge.

TO FREEZE Not suitable.

White chocolate mousses ᵛ

Really fast to make and memorable to eat.

Makes 8

BASE	WHITE CHOCOLATE MOUSSE
40g (1½ oz) plain Bournville chocolate	1 × 200g bar Continental white
75g (3 oz) Hobnob biscuits (without	chocolate, broken into small pieces
chocolate coating), coarsely crushed	200ml (7 fl oz) double cream,
225g (8 oz) strawberries, thinly sliced	lightly whipped
fresh mint sprigs	200ml (7 fl oz) full-fat crème fraîche

You will need eight 7cm (2 ¾ in) metal rings. Place on a baking sheet lined with non-stick baking paper.

1 Break the plain chocolate into a medium-sized bowl and melt over a pan of gently simmering water. Do not allow the chocolate to become too hot. Add the biscuits to the warm melted chocolate, stir to mix, then using the back of a metal spoon press into the bottom of the metal rings. Allow to set in the fridge.

2 For the mousse, break the white chocolate into a bowl and carefully melt over a pan of hot water. (Do not allow the chocolate to get too hot or it will become grainy; it should be slightly hotter than lukewarm.) Stir until smooth. Set aside to cool a little to firm up. Stir into the whipped cream and add the crème fraîche. Carefully mix until smooth.

3 Neatly arrange the strawberry slices up the sides of the rings and spoon the mousse mixture on to the individual biscuit bases. Gently level the tops. Chill until firm. Transfer to a plate, remove from the rings and decorate with mint.

cook now, eat later

TO PREPARE AHEAD Make up to 12 hours ahead, cover and keep in their rings in the fridge.

TO FREEZE Not suitable.

TO 'COOK' IN THE AGA Melt the chocolates in separate bowls on a tea-towel at the back of the Aga several hours ahead.

TIP If you haven't any metal rings, use small empty chopped tomato or baked bean cans. Take off the top and base with a can opener and wash thoroughly.

Lavender crème caramel ^V

Make this classic with a twist the day before and turn out when serving, or the caramel will lose its colour. And, if you turn the caramel custard out too soon, the caramel stays in the bottom of the dish. This recipe also makes 6 small ramekins. Do not use a non-stick pan to make the caramel – it will not work!

Serves 6

butter for greasing	CARAMEL
4 eggs	100g (4 oz) granulated sugar
25g (1 oz) caster sugar	4 tablespoons water
600ml (1 pint) milk	
3–4 tablespoons fresh lavender leaves	
(pull off the stalk) or flowers	

Preheat the oven to 150°C/300°F/Gas 2. Warm a 1.1 litre (2 pint) straight-sided round dish (a small soufflé dish is ideal) in the oven.

1 First make the caramel. Measure the granulated sugar and water into a clean stainless-steel pan. Dissolve the sugar slowly, stirring with a wooden spoon. When there are no sugar granules left, stop stirring and boil for a few minutes until the sugar turns a golden straw colour. Remove from the heat and pour quickly into the base of the warmed dish. Leave until cool then butter around the sides above the level of the caramel.

2 Whisk the eggs with the caster sugar in a bowl until well mixed.

3 Pour the milk into a saucepan with the lavender leaves or flowers and gently heat until you can still just dip your finger in for a moment, then strain through muslin on to the egg mixture. Stir and pour into the buttered dish.

4 Stand the dish in a small roasting tin and fill the tin half-way with boiling water. Cook in the oven for 40–50 minutes or until the custard has set. Do not overcook the custard – check around the edge of the dish to make sure no bubbles are appearing.

5 When cool, put into the fridge overnight so that the caramel is absorbed into the custard.

6 To serve, place a plate (with a lip, as the caramel will spread) on top of the dish and turn upside down. Serve with pouring cream.

cook now, eat later

TO PREPARE AND COOK AHEAD Make the day before and keep in the fridge. Turn out just before serving.

TO FREEZE Not suitable.

TO COOK IN THE AGA To make the caramel, warm the soufflé dish on the floor of the Simmering Oven for about 5–10 minutes. Dissolve the sugar and water in a pan on the Simmering Plate, stirring all the time until the sugar has dissolved. Take the spoon out of the pan and transfer the pan to the Boiling Plate. Boil rapidly until a golden straw colour. Finish step 1.

To cook the custard, follow the rest of the recipe to the end of step 3. Place the soufflé dish in a small roasting tin lined with kitchen paper. Half fill with boiling water and carefully transfer to the third set of runners in the Roasting Oven for about 12–15 minutes until the custard is just set, but still has a wobble. Carefully transfer to the Simmering Oven for a further 45–60 minutes, or until set.

TIP To make a caramel without the sugar crystallising, you must use a pan of stainless-steel, aluminium, enamel or copper. Never use a non-stick pan, which always seems to crystallise the sugar (and if it's got a dark lining, you can't *see* what is happening). Gently dissolve the sugar in the water, stirring with a wooden spoon. When the sugar has dissolved, discard the spoon, then boil rapidly until a pale caramel colour. If you let it get too dark, it will be bitter.

Lemon balm ice-cream ^V

Fresh ice-cream for hot summer days. If you are unable to get lemon balm, use ginger mint or fresh mint, or leave the herb out — it will still be lovely! Using this recipe you do not need an ice-cream maker or to re-whisk — it is just one process.

Serves 8–10

4 eggs, separated
finely grated zest and juice of 2 lemons
2 generous tablespoons lemon curd
2 tablespoons finely chopped fresh
   lemon balm
300ml (½ pint) pouring double cream
100g (4 oz) caster sugar

TO SERVE
fresh raspberries or raspberry coulis
fresh lemon balm

1 Whisk the egg yolks with the lemon zest and juice until well blended, then add the lemon curd and lemon balm. (This mixture is not very thick, don't worry.)

2 In a separate bowl, whisk the cream until it forms soft peaks. Fold the egg yolks and lemon mixture into the cream.

3 In a clean bowl, whisk the egg whites until stiff and gradually add the sugar, 1 teaspoon at a time, whisking continuously to form a stiff, shiny meringue mixture.

4 Gently fold the lemon cream into the egg white meringue mixture. Turn the ice-cream into a 1.4 litre (2½ pint) freezer container, cover, label and freeze overnight.

5 Serve in scoopfuls with fresh raspberries or raspberry coulis, decorated with more lemon balm.

cook now, eat later

TO PREPARE AHEAD AND FREEZE Prepare and freeze for up to 1 month.

Melon sorbet ^V

For a special occasion, use an orange-fleshed Cantaloupe or Charentais melon. They are expensive but have a wonderful flavour and colour.

Serves 8

1 large Ogen or Galia melon	pared rind and juice of 1 lemon
225g (8 oz) granulated sugar	300ml (½ pint) water
5 tablespoons water	

1 Cut the melon into quarters. Remove the skin and seeds and process the flesh until smooth.

2 Measure the sugar, 5 tablespoons water and the lemon rind into a medium heavy-based saucepan. Dissolve slowly over a gentle heat. When the sugar has completely dissolved, boil rapidly until the syrup is tacky and a short thread can be formed if the syrup is pulled between 2 teaspoons. Carefully remove and discard the lemon rind.

3 Mix together the melon purée, lemon juice, 300ml (½ pint) water and the warm syrup. Allow to cool.

4 Freeze the mixture overnight or until icy, then whisk until smooth and return to the freezer. (Or use an ice-cream machine if you have one, following the manufacturer's instructions.) Serve in well-chilled goblets.

cook now, eat later

TO PREPARE AHEAD AND FREEZE Prepare and freeze for up to 1 month.

Orange curd ice-cream with passionfruit and orange V

There are some delicious flavours here. When buying ready-made curds, check the labels to see that the contents are just butter, sugar and eggs, and no E numbers.

Serves 8–10

4 eggs, separated
100g (4 oz) caster sugar
300ml (½ pint) double cream, lightly
   whipped
finely grated zest of 1 medium orange
6 tablespoons luxury orange curd
fresh mint leaves to decorate

PASSIONFRUIT AND ORANGE
1–1½ oranges per person
¼ passionfruit per person

1 Place the egg yolks in a small bowl and whisk until well blended. Using an electric hand whisk, whisk the egg whites until stiff, then whisk in the sugar 1 teaspoon at a time until stiff and glossy.

2 Fold the cream into the egg yolks, with the orange zest and curd. Mix in 1 spoonful of egg white and carefully fold in the remaining egg white.

3 Turn the ice-cream into a 1.4 litre (2½ pint) plastic container, cover and freeze overnight.

4 Segment the oranges. Cut each passionfruit in half, and scoop out the pulp. Mix together.

5 Serve the tangy fruit mixture with the orange curd ice-cream, and decorate with mint.

cook now, eat later

> **TO PREPARE AHEAD AND FREEZE** Prepare and freeze the ice-cream for up to 1 month. Prepare the oranges and passionfruit, cover and keep in the fridge for up to 24 hours. Remove the ice-cream from the freezer 5–10 minutes before serving and leave to stand at room temperature.

Clockwise from top left: Lemon Balm Ice-cream; Melon Sorbet;
Orange Curd Ice-cream with Passionfruit and Orange

Five-fruit salad ^V

This is a lovely fresh fruit salad. Do not add any sugar, just enjoy the natural sweetness from the fruit juices. I often serve this if the main pudding is very rich. If any is left, the fruits are delicious for breakfast.

Serves 6

1 melon	1 papaya (paw-paw)
2 mangoes	225g (8 oz) raspberries
1 pink grapefruit	

1 First prepare the melon. Using a sharp knife, cut into quarters and remove the pips. Remove the skin by slipping the knife between the flesh and the skin, then chop into large pieces.

2 Peel the mangoes. Cut a thick slice from either side of the stone, then chop the flesh into large cubes.

3 Using a knife with a serrated edge, peel and segment the grapefruit, saving any juice.

4 Peel the papaya, take out the seeds with a teaspoon, and cut the flesh into pieces.

5 Put all the prepared fruit, except for the raspberries, in a bowl, cover with clingfilm and put in the fridge, mixing from time to time.

6 Just before serving, add the fresh raspberries. Serve with crème fraîche if liked.

cook now, eat later

TO PREPARE AHEAD The bulk of the salad can be made the day before. Just add the raspberries at the last minute.

TO FREEZE Not suitable.

COOKING FOR A CROWD

When cooking for a large number, you need to get down to planning as soon as you can. Think carefully about what sort of party it will be. If people are to stand to eat, they need something that can be cut with a fork alone. If you offer something like gammon, they'll need a knife and fork, and will have to sit down. Is it to be a buffet party, with cold foods and salads laid out on a table for everyone to help themselves, or will you be offering something hot, which you help them to? Ask for help and tell your helper a certain dish will serve 8 or 10, perhaps even indicating portion sizes on the dish itself.

When still at the planning stages, consider who your guests are and at what time of day the party is to be held. If they've had a long time standing and chatting, and it's a long time since breakfast or lunch, they'll probably be hungry and eat a lot – this is particularly true of younger guests! But if it's a lunch or supper party at the end of the Christmas holiday, nobody will be interested in eating too much . . .

When planning a cold buffet party, the gammon will look very impressive (and you can cook it 6 days ahead!). The *Cockatrice* (page 196) will astound everyone and, although it's complicated to assemble initially, it can be done in advance. It's best cold, and the cooking can be done two days in advance. My carving ideas concerning fillet of beef will open your eyes to its buffet potential – no more grey, unappetising slices lying limply on the plate. And never over-do the salad choice either. Stick to a couple only, rather than overwhelming your guests with potential flavours and texture. If serving a pie such as the steak and mushroom one on page 200, do so in a shallow dish so that everyone gets a bit of the crispy potato topping.

Once you have decided on the type of party and on what you plan to cook, you can order ingredients well in advance, cook, chill and freeze (if appropriate). Everything in this chapter can be prepared in advance.

Three Bean, Tomato and Asparagus Salad **V**

Herb and Parmesan Soft Rolls **V**

Peppadew and Cheddar Scone Bake **V**

Glazed Apple Gammon

Salmon and Fennel Fish Pie

Reggiori Pasta Bake with Tuna and Two Cheeses

Chilled Gazpacho Chicken

Cockatrice

The Perfect Whole Roast Fillet of Beef with Thyme

Steak and Mushroom Pie with Dauphinoise Potato Topping

Lancashire Lamb Shanks

For other ideas, see:

Any of the recipes in the other sections,
and simply double the ingredients.

Three bean, tomato and asparagus salad ^V

This can be made ahead completely as the beans can marinate in the dressing and the tomatoes will not lose too much liquid. Serve on a stylish platter for your buffet table.

Serves 10–12

1 × 400g can lentils	225g (8 oz) asparagus tips
1 × 400g can flageolet beans	10 tomatoes, skinned and sliced
1 × 400g can black-eyed beans	1 tablespoon balsamic vinegar and
4 spring onions, sliced on the diagonal	2 tablespoons olive oil, mixed
6 tablespoons good salad dressing	a handful of freshly snipped chives and
salt and freshly ground black pepper	torn basil leaves

1 Drain and rinse the lentils and beans. Pat dry on kitchen paper, then mix together in a bowl. Stir in the spring onions, salad dressing and salt and pepper. Arrange along the base of a thin flat dish.

2 Blanch the asparagus tips in boiling salted water for about 2–3 minutes until just tender, drain and refresh in cold water. Dry on kitchen paper.

3 Arrange the tomato slices over the beans, overlapping. Arrange the asparagus tips in a herringbone shape along the centre of the tomatoes.

4 Season with salt and pepper, then drizzle the balsamic vinegar and oil mixture over the whole dish. Sprinkle over the chives and basil, and serve.

cook now, eat later

> **TO PREPARE AHEAD** Make completely to the end of step 3 up to some 12 hours ahead.
>
> **TO FREEZE** Not suitable.

Herb and Parmesan soft rolls ^V

This is a quick and easy way of making rolls. You can make them by hand or use a dough hook which will save time and effort. This recipe can also be used to make two small 450g (1 lb) loaves, but naturally they will take a little longer to bake.

Makes 20 rolls

500g (1 lb 2 oz) strong white flour, plus
   extra for kneading

4 tablespoons olive oil, plus extra for
   glazing

350ml (12 fl oz) warm water

3 teaspoons salt

1 × 7g packet fast-action yeast

50g (2 oz) Parmesan, freshly grated, plus
   extra for sprinkling

25g (1 oz) fresh chives, snipped

a good handful of fresh basil leaves,
   chopped

a good handful of fresh parsley, chopped

sunflower seeds

1 Measure the flour, oil, water, salt and yeast into the mixer and mix using the dough hook for 5–8 minutes – the mixture will look quite wet – or mix by hand. Put into a large oiled bowl covered with clingfilm. Place in the fridge overnight.

2 The next day take the dough out of the fridge. It should have doubled in bulk. Leave the dough on one side for 1 hour to bring back to room temperature, then knock back by kneading in the mixer or on a floured surface for 5 minutes by hand.

3 Add the cheese and herbs and continue to knead until they are well incorporated. Divide the dough into 20 pieces and roll into balls. Place these close together on a greased baking sheet, and cover with an oiled plastic bag. (A cleaners' suit plastic bag is ideal – just tie a knot in the plastic where the hanger hole is.) Leave to prove in a warm place for about 30 minutes until the rolls have doubled in size.

Meanwhile, preheat the oven to 200°C/400°F/Gas 6.

4 Lightly glaze the rolls with oil and sprinkle with sunflower seeds and Parmesan. Bake in the preheated oven for about 20–25 minutes until well risen, golden and the rolls sound hollow when tapped on the base. Best served warm.

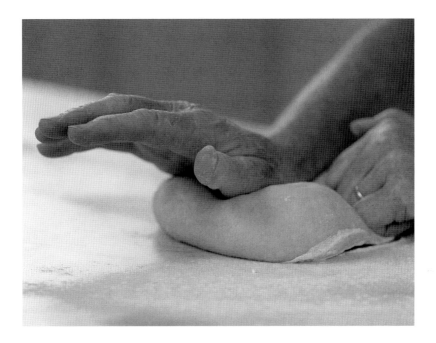

cook now, eat later

TO PREPARE AND COOK AHEAD Complete step 1 the day before. Or the rolls can be baked the day before they are needed and then refreshed in a moderate oven at 180°C/350°F/Gas 4 for 15 minutes when required.

TO FREEZE Cool the cooked rolls completely, pack into a plastic bag and freeze for up to 3 months. Thaw at room temperature. Refresh in a moderate oven as above for about 10–15 minutes.

TO COOK IN THE AGA Bake the rolls for about 20–30 minutes on the grid shelf on the floor of the Roasting Oven. Check after 15 minutes. Remove the grid shelf and put the baking sheet directly on the floor of the Roasting Oven to brown the bases.

Peppadew and Cheddar scone bake ^V

Lovely for a lunch box or with soup or salad. Serve with butter or cream cheese. These can be cut into more than 12 pieces if you want a smaller slice.

Makes 12 squares

450g (1 lb) self-raising flour	225g (8 oz) mature Cheddar, grated
4 teaspoons baking powder	100g (4 oz) peppadew bell peppers,
1 teaspoon salt	drained and finely sliced
½ teaspoon mustard powder	2 eggs
freshly ground black pepper	milk
100g (4 oz) butter, at room temperature	

Lightly grease a 30 × 23cm (12 × 9 in) traybake tin or roasting tin. Preheat the oven to 230°C/450°F/Gas 8.

1 Measure the flour, baking powder, salt and mustard powder into a large bowl and add a little black pepper. Add the butter and rub into the flour using the fingertips until the mixture resembles fine breadcrumbs. Stir in the cheese and peppers.

2 Break the eggs into a measuring jug, beat together, and make up to 300ml (½ pint) with milk. Add to the flour mixture, mixing to form a soft dough.

3 Knead the dough quickly and lightly until smooth, then roll out on a lightly floured work surface to an oblong to fit the roasting tin. Mark into 12 squares and brush the top with a little milk.

4 Bake in the preheated oven for about 20 minutes until the scone is well risen and golden. Turn out on to a wire rack to cool. Break apart to serve.

cook now, eat later

TO PREPARE AND COOK AHEAD Bake up to 24 hours in advance, then reheat and refresh in the tin in a moderate oven at 180°C/350°F/Gas 4 for about 10 minutes.

TO FREEZE Allow the baked scone to cool completely, then pack into a strong polythene bag and freeze for up to 3 months. Thaw at room temperature and reheat and refresh in a moderate oven as above to serve.

TO COOK IN THE AGA Slide the traybake tin on to the grid shelf on the floor of the Roasting Oven for about 15 minutes or until a perfect golden brown. Slide the plain cold sheet on to the second set of runners and bake for a further 5–10 minutes until firm and shrinking away from the sides of the tin.

Glazed apple gammon

There is nothing like home-cooked ham for Christmas or for a buffet. For a change we have cooked this one in apple juice which complements the meat perfectly (use the sort you buy in cartons). If you buy gammon from the butcher, it may be a special cure and need soaking before cooking – ask his advice. Supermarket gammons do not usually need soaking.

Serves 20 at least

4kg (9 lb) half gammon, unsmoked	2 generous tablespoons redcurrant jelly
2 litres (3½ pints) apple juice	I tablespoon Dijon mustard

1 Place the gammon in a large pan just big enough to hold it, and cover with the apple juice. Bring to the boil over a high heat. Turn the heat down to simmer, cover and cook very gently for about 4 hours (55 minutes per kg, 25 minutes per lb) until tender. I advise using a meat thermometer (the thermometer should read 75°C when done), but put it in at the end as it must not be submerged in liquid. To test for doneness without a thermometer, pierce the gammon with a skewer – it should feel tender as the skewer goes into the meat.

2 Allow the meat to cool in the liquid. Remove from the pan, and place on a piece of foil in a small roasting tin. Gently remove the skin, leaving the fat on top. Melt the redcurrant jelly, stir in the mustard and spread evenly over the fat of the ham. Score the glaze diagonally with a sharp knife, cutting through the fat. Wrap the lean meat in foil.

3 Glaze and brown under the grill or glaze in a preheated oven at 220°C/425°F/Gas 7 until golden brown and crisp – about 15 minutes.

4 If serving cold, chill in the fridge for 12 hours or so before carving.

cook now, eat later

TO PREPARE AND COOK AHEAD The completed gammon can be made up to 6 days ahead and kept in the fridge.

TO FREEZE Not suitable.

TO COOK IN THE AGA Bring to the boil on the Boiling Plate, cover and transfer to the Simmering Oven for about 4–5 hours (depending on your Simmering Oven) until tender. Glaze at step 3 in a roasting tin on the highest set of runners in the Roasting Oven until golden brown and crisp.

Salmon and fennel fish pie

This is a fish pie for a very special occasion. Adding ricotta cheese to the mashed potato lightens the texture and gives an interesting flavour.

Serves 12

700g (1½ lb) fresh fennel bulbs

300ml (½ pint) dry white wine

about 800ml (1½ pints) hot milk

100g (4 oz) butter

100g (4 oz) plain flour

salt and freshly ground black pepper

1.4kg (3 lb) salmon fillet, skinned and cut into 1cm (½ in) pieces

2 tablespoons chopped fresh dill

8 eggs, hard boiled and cut into eighths

TOPPING

1.6kg (3½ lb) King Edward potatoes (weight before peeling), peeled and cut into large chunks

500g (1 lb 2 oz) ricotta cheese

about 8 tablespoons milk

100g (4 oz) Parmesan, freshly grated

You will need one shallow ovenproof dish, capacity 3 litres (5 pints), about 35 × 25 × 5cm (14 × 10 × 2 in), or two shallow ovenproof dishes, capacity 1.4 litres (2½ pints), about 28 × 23 × 5cm (11 × 9 × 2 in). Preheat the oven to 200°C/400°F/Gas 6.

1 For the topping, cook the potatoes in boiling salted water until tender. Drain well.

2 Whilst the potatoes are cooking, cut the fennel bulbs in half from top to bottom, and remove and discard the core. Cut into quarters and then slice in horseshoe shapes. Put into a small pan with the wine, and simmer until the fennel is soft, about 10 minutes. Drain the fennel, reserving the liquid, and make up to 1.1 litres (2 pints) with the milk.

3 Next make the sauce. Melt the butter in a medium pan, add the flour and stir to mix. Gradually add the milk and fennel liquid, stirring continuously, and allowing to thicken. Season well, bring to the boil, and simmer for a few minutes, then add the salmon pieces and cook for a further few minutes. Stir in the fennel and dill, check the seasoning, and spread into the dish or dishes. Scatter the eggs over the sauce. Press down gently into the fish mixture.

4 Mash the potatoes until smooth. Stir in the ricotta cheese, adding enough milk to give a creamy texture, and plenty of salt and pepper. Spoon over the fish and sauce, spreading the potatoes right to the edge of the dish. Sprinkle with the Parmesan.

5 Bake in the preheated oven for about 30–35 minutes until cooked through, brown and crisp and piping hot. If using two dishes, change the dishes around half-way through the cooking time if necessary.

recipe continued overleaf

Reggiori pasta bake with tuna and two cheeses

Rigatoni is large tube-shaped pasta, ideal for use in a baked pasta dish such as this one.

Serves 12

1 large onion, coarsely chopped	a little paprika
350g (12 oz) dried rigatoni pasta	
2 × 400g cans tuna in brine, drained well	CHEESE SAUCE
2–3 tablespoons capers, drained and	100g (4 oz) butter
roughly chopped	100g (4 oz) plain flour
2 tablespoons snipped fresh chives	1.1 litres (2 pints) milk
4 large tomatoes, about 400g (14 oz),	2 teaspoons Dijon mustard
skinned and roughly chopped	4 tablespoons chopped fresh parsley
salt and freshly ground black pepper	50g (2 oz) mozzarella cheese, grated
150ml (¼ pint) double cream	50g (2 oz) Gruyère cheese, grated

Preheat the oven to 200°C/400°F/Gas 6. You will need two 28 × 23 × 5 cm (11 × 9 × 2 in) shallow ovenproof dishes, lightly buttered.

▌ Cook the onion in boiling salted water with the pasta until al dente. Drain and refresh with cold water until completely cold. Drain well then divide between the prepared ovenproof dishes.

2 Next make the sauce. Melt the butter in a large pan, take off the heat and stir in the flour. Gradually add the milk, stirring continuously, and bring to the boil. Season with salt, pepper and mustard, and simmer for 2 minutes. Add the parsley and half of each cheese. Stir to mix.

3 Mix the tuna, capers, chives and tomatoes in a bowl and season well with salt and pepper. Spoon over the pasta in the dishes, spreading the tuna out evenly. Pour the cheese sauce over the tuna mixture in the dishes.

4 Next pour over the cream and scatter over the remaining cheeses. Sprinkle with paprika.

5 Bake in the preheated oven for about 30 minutes until the top is golden and bubbling.

cook now, eat later

TO PREPARE AND COOK AHEAD Prepare to the end of step 3 up to 24 hours ahead. Cool, cover and keep in the fridge. Complete steps 4 and 5 to serve.

TO FREEZE Add 150ml (¼ pint) more milk to the cheese sauce if you wish to freeze the pasta bake after step 3. Don't pour over the cream or scatter with the cheese yet. Cover and freeze for up to 1 month. Thaw overnight in the fridge. Complete step 4 and heat as in step 5, increasing the time to about 40 minutes, or until piping hot.

TO COOK IN THE AGA Bake the assembled dish on the grid shelf on the floor of the Roasting Oven for about 25 minutes.

Chilled gazpacho chicken

Gazpacho is an old favourite cold soup for summer. I have combined the raw ingredients with cooked chicken to make an up-to-date Coronation chicken. You can of course use cooked turkey instead of the chicken.

Serves 12 (as part of a buffet)

2 medium chickens, cooked (yielding about 900g/2 lb flesh)

200ml (7 fl oz) 'light' low-calorie mayonnaise

200ml (7 fl oz) full-fat crème fraîche

4 tablespoons sun-dried tomato paste

18–20 peppadew bell peppers, drained and thinly sliced

2 garlic cloves, crushed

12 spring onions, white part only, thinly sliced

4 teaspoons balsamic vinegar

4 tablespoons chopped fresh basil, plus a handful of leaves to garnish

salt and freshly ground black pepper

GARNISH SALAD

2 small cucumbers, peeled, seeded and cut into pieces

500g (1 lb 2 oz) cherry tomatoes, cut in half

100g (4 oz) black olives (the best are in olive oil from the deli counter)

chopped fresh parsley

a little French dressing

1 Cut the chicken into neat bite-sized pieces, removing all the skin and bone.

2 Mix the mayonnaise and crème fraîche with the tomato paste, peppers and garlic. Fold in the chicken pieces and spring onions, then taste and season carefully with the balsamic vinegar, basil, salt and pepper.

3 Spoon out on to a flat serving dish and garnish with the dressed salad and basil leaves.

cook now, eat later

TO PREPARE AHEAD Prepare the chicken to the end of step 2, cover and keep in the fridge for up to 24 hours ahead. The garnish salad can be prepared up to 12 hours ahead, but do not dress. Spoon the chicken on to a flat serving dish and garnish with the salad and fresh basil.

TO FREEZE Not suitable.

TIP Peppadew peppers are small bell peppers from South Africa, found in jars in good delis and supermarkets. They are available hot or mild, and we like the mild ones best. Once opened, keep in the fridge, and use them in salads, pasta, stuffed with cream cheese, and in any of the recipes here (see pages 188 and 252).

Cockatrice

Three birds in one. The earliest mention of this idea I have found is in Elizabeth Raffald's English Housekeeper *in 1769. It was called 'Yorkshire Goose Pie' and consisted of many boned birds, one inside the other, a goose, then a turkey, then 2 ducks and then a few woodcocks. It was then covered with pastry and baked for 4 hours and then 2 pounds of butter were poured on top of the pie. It was served cold. Ours is a healthier, simpler version!*

This variation of Cockatrice was given to me recently in Guernsey by Steve Halstead, the senior chef lecturer at the catering college. He and some of his students gave me great support when I was demonstrating on the island. I've never had my herbs chopped at such speed!

Ask your butcher to bone the birds for you and give him plenty of notice; you can freeze them ahead. Thaw thoroughly before stuffing and assembling the Cockatrice. Ask him for the bones and giblets for gravy. There is no need to tunnel-bone the birds — cutting down the backbone makes it easier to assemble. If you wish to freeze the raw completed Cockatrice, use fresh boned birds, not frozen. Cockatrice can be served hot with port gravy, but we prefer it cold. If you can't get frozen chestnuts, use 100g (4 oz) dried chestnuts soaked overnight.

Serves 20

1 x 5.5kg (12 lb) turkey, boned and last
    drumstick bone left in
1 x 2.5kg (5½ lb) duck, boned
1 x 1kg (2¼ lb) chicken, boned
salt and freshly ground black pepper
plenty of butter, softened

STUFFING
2 onions, finely chopped
50g (2 oz) butter
175g (6 oz) streaky bacon, snipped
225g (8 oz) frozen chestnuts, thawed
    and roughly chopped
50g (2 oz) fresh white breadcrumbs
2 tablespoons dried sage

225g (8 oz) spinach, chopped, or 450g
    (1lb) frozen chopped spinach, thawed
    and drained
450g (1 lb) good pork sausages, skinned
1 egg

PORT GRAVY (IF SERVING HOT)
50g (2 oz) butter
1 onion, roughly chopped
50g (2 oz) plain flour
150ml (¼ pint) red wine or port
1.1 litres (2 pints) stock made from the
    chicken and turkey bones
1–2 tablespoons cranberry or
    redcurrant jelly

Preheat the oven to 220°C/425°F/Gas 7.

❚ First make the stuffing. Cook the onion in the butter until soft, without colouring. Add the bacon and chestnuts. Stir from time to time until lightly browned. Remove from the heat and add the breadcrumbs, sage and spinach. Allow to become cold. Mix in the sausages, egg and 1 teaspoon each of salt and pepper. I find it easiest to mix using my hands.

2 Lay each bird, breast side down, on the work surface. Trim the excess fat from the duck, and season well inside each bird.

3 Take a quarter of the stuffing and stuff the chicken, then re-shape roughly. Spread another quarter of stuffing liberally over the duck and put the stuffed chicken inside the duck. Wrap up neatly in an approximation of its former shape. There is no need to sew up either of the birds. Repeat with the remaining stuffing and turkey. You can sew up the Cockatrice but I find it much easier to use skewers. Shape it to look as much like a plain turkey as possible. Tie 3 lengths of string around the bird and 1 from end to end. Also tie the legs together.

4 Butter the turkey breast well, and put a meat thermometer into the centre of the Cockatrice. Wrap loosely in foil and roast in the preheated oven for about 1 hour. Lower the temperature to 160°C/325°F/Gas 3, and cook for a further 2 hours until the thermometer reads 75°C. You can also test with a skewer: the juices should run clear. It is essential not to undercook. Increase the oven temperature to 220°C/425°F/Gas 7, open the foil and brown the breasts of the bird, about 10 minutes. Rest or cool if serving cold.

5 For the gravy if serving hot, heat the butter, add the onion and cook slowly until lightly browned. Stir in the flour, scraping well on the bottom of the pan, then pour in the red wine or port and allow to reduce slightly. Slowly stir in the stock and add cranberry or redcurrant jelly to taste. Bring to the boil and season.

6 To serve the Cockatrice hot, allow to rest with a covering of foil – this will make carving easier and allow the juices to settle. Carve straight across the bird taking slices from the end first. Sadly it does not hold together very well when served hot but it tastes delicious.

7 To serve the Cockatrice cold, roast 2 days ahead, cool and refrigerate. To carve, cut in half across the middle then cut the back end in half again. Cut fairly thick slices from these two quarters to start with. Serve with *Scarlet Confit* (see page 227).

cook now, eat later

TO PREPARE AND COOK AHEAD Stuff and wrap the raw bird in foil in the fridge 1 day ahead. Roast and cook completely 2 days ahead, cool well and refrigerate.

TO FREEZE Freeze for up to 1 month raw. Thaw for 2 days in the fridge.

TO COOK IN THE AGA At step 4 roast in the Roasting Oven on the grid shelf on the floor for about 1 hour then transfer to the Simmering Oven for about 1½ hours until done (longer if you have a slow Simmering Oven).

The perfect whole roast fillet of beef with thyme

Cold rare roast fillet of beef is sheer luxury for a special occasion. So often a beautifully cooked fillet is carved too early, arranged on a platter and in an hour or so after exposing the cut surface to the air the meat turns grey – so disappointing. However, a very easy solution is to carve the cold fillet up to 6 hours ahead and then reassemble it back into a roast fillet shape and to tightly wrap it in clingfilm. Then just arrange it on the platter immediately before serving. Ask the butcher to tie the joint neatly so that it keeps its round shape during roasting.

If you like very hot horseradish, use hot horseradish instead of the creamed. For me, life is too short to grate fresh horseradish!

Serves 8–12
(depending upon whether you are serving other cold meats as well)

1.5kg (3 lb) fillet of beef, cut from the thick end	HORSERADISH SAUCE
	generous ½ × 185g jar horseradish cream
12 large sprigs of fresh thyme	3 tablespoons whipped or thick cream
3 garlic cloves, crushed	
3 tablespoons olive oil	
salt and freshly ground black pepper	

1 First marinate the beef for 24 hours. Put the fillet into a strong polythene bag with the thyme, garlic, oil and pepper. Keep in the fridge in the marinade for up to 24 hours.

Preheat the oven to 220°C/425°F/Gas 7.

2 Heat a non-stick frying pan until hot. Lift the thyme out of the marinade and put to one side. Seal the beef on all sides using the oil from the marinade in the hot frying pan. When gloriously brown lift out on to foil in a roasting tin and sprinkle with salt.

3 Roast in the preheated oven for 30 minutes (10 minutes per 450g/1 lb). The internal temperature should be 60°C for rare if you use a meat thermometer. (Not quite so rare, 62–63°C.)

4 Leave to become completely cold before carving (see introduction).

5 A nice garnish is to fry the fresh thyme, which makes it bright green, or just decorate with parsley. Serve with the horseradish sauce made from a mixture of the horseradish cream and whipped cream.

recipe continued overleaf

cook now, eat later

Steak and mushroom pie with dauphinoise potato topping

Few people have a large enough dish for 12, so you can make this in two 30 × 23 × 6cm (12 × 9 × 2½ in) if preferred. It is important to part-cook the potatoes ahead, otherwise they will go black.

Serves 12

2kg (4½ lb) good stewing steak, cut into 2.5cm (1 in) cubes
sunflower oil
4 large onions, roughly chopped
700g (1½ lb) small open (dark-gilled) mushrooms, sliced
a good 4 tablespoons plain flour
about 1.1 litres (2 pints) beef stock
2 tablespoons Worcestershire sauce
salt and freshly ground black pepper
a little gravy browning (optional)

DAUPHINOISE POTATO TOPPING
2.2kg (4¾ lb) old potatoes, peeled
about 100g (4 oz) butter, melted
150g (5 oz) Cheddar, grated

You will need a shallow ovenproof dish, about 38 × 28 × 8cm (15 × 11 × 3 in).

1 Brown the meat, in batches, in a little oil in a large frying pan, over a high heat. Remove from the pan.

2 Add the onion to the pan, fry for a couple of minutes, then lower the heat and simmer for about 10 minutes until soft. Add the mushrooms and flour. Cook, stirring, for 1 minute then add the stock, Worcestershire sauce, seasoning and a little gravy browning if liked. Bring to the boil, and allow to thicken, stirring until smooth.

3 Return the meat to the pan, bring back to the boil, then cover and simmer very gently for about 2 hours, until the meat is tender. (Or cook in the oven preheated to 160°C/325°F/Gas 3 until tender, perhaps nearer 3 hours.)

4 For the topping, cook the potatoes in boiling salted water until just tender. Cool a little, then slice thickly and toss in the melted butter.

Preheat the oven to 200°C/400°F/Gas 6.

5 Spoon the meat into . Layer the potatoes on top, seasoning well in between the layers. Top with the cheese. Cook in the preheated oven for about 30 minutes until the cheese is bubbling and golden and the meat is hot through.

cook now, eat later

TO PREPARE AND COOK AHEAD Prepare and cook the steak to the end of step 3. Cool, cover and keep in the fridge for up to 2 days. Cook the potatoes, slice and toss in the melted butter earlier in the day. Assemble the pie as in step 5, then reheat until piping hot at the same temperature, allowing a little longer from cold.

TO FREEZE Freeze the cooked meat base only for up to 3 months. Thaw overnight, then assemble the pie, and reheat as above, allowing a little longer from cold.

TO COOK IN THE AGA Fry the onions and meat and make the gravy on the Boiling Plate. Transfer to the Simmering Oven, covered, for about 2½–3 hours or until tender. Continue steps 4 and 5. When the potato topping is added, cook at the top of the Roasting Oven for about 30 minutes until golden brown.

Lancashire lamb shanks

It is wonderful that we can buy lamb shanks so easily in supermarkets. They are often cooked with a tomato and red wine based sauce, so I have developed this recipe using a light sauce with white wine and herbs. Do cook the shanks really well until the meat falls off the bone. If you like crisper vegetables, add them to the stew for the last hour only.

Serves 12

12 lamb shanks, about 350g (12 oz) each in weight

salt and freshly ground black pepper

1 tablespoon sunflower oil

100g (4 oz) butter

175g (6 oz) plain flour

1.1 litres (2 pints) white wine

750ml (1¼ pints) good chicken or lamb stock

2 large onions, peeled and cut into eighths

2 large carrots, peeled, cut into 2.5cm (1 in) batons

2 butternut squashes, total weight 900g (2 lb), peeled and cut into 2.5cm (1 in) slices

masses of chopped fresh parsley

1 Heat a large frying pan. Season the lamb shanks with salt and pepper. Brown the shanks in the oil and butter on each side until golden brown (you will need to do this in batches). Transfer the shanks to a deep stewpan large enough to hold all 12 of them (and the vegetables).

2 Make the sauce in the original frying pan. Add the flour to the fat left in the pan. Mix together off the heat, return to the heat, and gradually add the wine and stock. Bring to the boil, stirring all the time, until the sauce boils and becomes thickish and smooth in consistency. Season with salt and pepper and pour this sauce over the shanks in the casserole.

3 Bring the sauce and shanks back to the boil, cover with the lid and simmer for about 1½ hours.

4 Add the vegetables, pushing them down so they are covered with the sauce, and bring back to the boil. Cover with the lid and simmer for a further 1–1½ hours or until the vegetables are just tender and the meat is falling off the bone. Check the seasoning. (If preferred, cook in a preheated slow oven at 160°C/325°F/Gas 3, following the same instructions as above.)

5 Stir in the parsley and serve with *Leek Mash* (see page 106).

cook now, eat later

TO PREPARE AND COOK AHEAD The whole casserole can be made up to 2 days before and kept covered in the fridge. Add the vegetables for slightly less time, as they will continue to cook when the casserole is reheated. Reheat gently so as not to break up the vegetables.

TO FREEZE Not suitable.

TO COOK IN THE AGA Brown the shanks on the Boiling Plate until golden brown. Cook from step 3 covered in the Simmering Oven for about 2–2½ hours or until the shanks are tender.

HOME BAKING

As you know, home baking is one of my passions, and I love creating new cakes, biscuits and traybakes. One of the principal advantages of home baking is that most cakes can be frozen: you can cool them, wrap them well and freeze as soon as possible after baking, and they will emerge as good as new after a couple of months. Cakes might need icing after defrosting (many icings look best when fresh), and scones and muffins will need to be oven-refreshed, but the basic work has all been done well in advance.

Baking needs to be a little more precise than many other aspects of cookery. For instance, it really is essential to weigh everything correctly. Usually people weigh 'heavy', so you should check your scales against a packet of sugar or butter. The right size of tin is essential as well: have a ruler or tape measure handy to check the width and depth of each tin. So often people say a particular sponge recipe hasn't worked, and it's turned out that they've used the wrong tin. It makes a huge difference.

And ingredients are very important too. Use natural sugars if you can, as they contain no dyes. All the recipes call for large eggs, and organic are best. Be careful with baking powder: if you use even fractionally too much, the cake will rise up then fall down again! Fats are a contentious issue now. The method I use for mixing cakes before baking is the all-in-one method. All the ingredients are put into the bowl then beaten together with a hand whisk until smooth. I once used baking margarines with an 80 per cent fat content, and these, like butter, would be slightly softened before mixing. However, these margarines seem to have disappeared from the market to a large extent for some reason, and I am often obliged to use spreads with a reduced fat content (70–73 per cent) instead, such as Stork Tub, Flora Original or Flora Buttery. Because of the reduced fat content, these need to be used straight from the fridge, otherwise they would be too soft and the cake mix would be too runny. Always look at the packaging: ideally you want 80 per cent fat margarine, to use at room temperature.

Ginger and Orange Cake with Mascarpone Icing **V**

Double Chocolate Chip Brownie Cake **V**

Lemon and Lime Traybake **V**

Banoffee Traybake **V**

Apricot and Brandy Cake **V**

Chocolate and Rum Cake **V**

Apricot and Walnut Breakfast Muffins **V**

Sultana Spice Traybake **V**

Orange Chocolate Shortbread Biscuits **V**

Fresh Raspberry Scones **V**

Mega Chocolate Cookies **V**

Apple and Lemon Drop Scones **V**

For more baking ideas, see:

Herb and Parmesan Soft Rolls (see page 186)

Peppadew and Cheddar Scone Bake (see page 188)

Frangipane Mince Pies (see page 232)

Classic Victorian Christmas Cake (see page 234)

Christmas Chocolate Log (see page 236)

Ginger and orange cake with mascarpone icing ᵛ

A delicious and light cake, best kept in the fridge because of the icing. This cake is a true favourite with all who work with me!

Cuts into 8–10 wedges

225g (8 oz) self-raising flour	4 eggs
2 level teaspoons baking powder	5–6 bulbs stem ginger in syrup, coarsely
225g (8 oz) baking margarine or butter,	chopped, plus syrup
at room temperature	finely grated zest of 1 orange
225g (8 oz) caster sugar	1 × 250g tub mascarpone cheese

Preheat the oven to 180°C/350°F/Gas 4. Base-line two 20cm (8 in) deep sandwich tins with non-stick paper, and grease well.

1 Measure the flour, baking powder, margarine or butter, sugar, eggs, 3–4 bulbs of the ginger and the grated orange zest into a large mixing bowl. Using an electric hand mixer, mix well until thoroughly blended. Divide the mixture evenly between the prepared tins and level out.

2 Bake in the centre of the preheated oven for 20–25 minutes until golden brown and shrinking away from the sides of the tin. Leave to cool for a few moments then turn out.

3 For the filling/icing, beat the mascarpone with 2 tablespoons of the ginger syrup. When the cakes are completely cold, sandwich with half of this mixture. Spread the remainder on top of the cake and sprinkle over the remaining coarsely chopped ginger.

cook now, eat later

TO PREPARE AND COOK AHEAD Make the cakes and store in an airtight container for up to 3 days before filling and icing. Make the filling/icing when you need it.

TO FREEZE The cakes freeze well un-iced. Wrap and freeze for up to 3 months. Thaw for about 4 hours at room temperature, then fill and ice.

TO COOK IN THE AGA 2-oven Aga: Bake on the grid shelf on the floor of the Roasting Oven with the cold shelf on the second set of runners for about 25 minutes. Turn half-way through baking.

4-oven Aga: Bake on the grid shelf on the floor of the Baking Oven for 25 minutes, sliding in the cold shelf on the second set of runners only if the cakes become too dark.

Double chocolate chip brownie cake ^V

A quick and easy chocolate cake. Making two loaves allows you to freeze one for another day.

Makes 2 loaves

100g (4 oz) ground almonds	2 level teaspoons baking powder
225g (8 oz) baking margarine or butter, at room temperature	150g (5 oz) white chocolate buttons
175g (6 oz) self-raising flour	ICING
225g (8 oz) light muscovado sugar	200g (7 oz) dark chocolate (Bournville)
50g (2 oz) cocoa powder	50g (2 oz) butter
5 eggs	25g (1 oz) white chocolate buttons

Grease and line two 450g (1 lb) loaf tins (top measurement 17 × 11cm/6½ × 4 in). Preheat the oven to 180°C/350°F/Gas 4.

1 Measure all the ingredients for the cake, except the white buttons, into a bowl and mix until smooth. Fold in the white chocolate buttons and pour into the tins. Level the surface.

2 Bake in the middle of the preheated oven for about 1 hour or until well risen, firm to the touch and shrinking away from the sides of the tin. Allow the cakes to cool on a wire rack.

3 For the icing, put the dark chocolate and butter into a bowl. Place over a pan of simmering water to melt. Stir, leave for 2 minutes, then spread over the top of the cakes. Dot the white chocolate buttons on to the warm chocolate icing.

cook now, eat later

TO PREPARE AND COOK AHEAD Bake and ice, up to 3 days ahead. The icing, though, is better made nearer the time of serving.

TO FREEZE Cool, pack and freeze the un-iced cakes for up to 3 months. Thaw at room temperature for about 4 hours. Ice as directed in the recipe.

TO COOK IN THE AGA 2-oven Aga: Place the tins on the grill rack in the large roasting tin. Slide on to the lowest set of runners in the Roasting Oven with the cold sheet on the second set of runners. Bake for about 30 minutes until the cakes are well risen and set. Carefully transfer to the Simmering Oven for about 25 minutes.

4-oven Aga: Place the tins on the grill rack in the large roasting tin. Slide on to the lowest set of runners in the Baking Oven for about 35–45 minutes. Check half-way through cooking: if too brown, slide the cold sheet on to the second set of runners.

For the icing, melt chocolate and butter in Simmering Oven for about 10 minutes.

Lemon and lime traybake ^V

For a special occasion, or if the limes are a reasonable price, you could use the juice and zest of 6 limes for a really fresh taste, omitting the lemon.

Cuts into 21 pieces

275g (10 oz) self-raising flour
225g (8 oz) caster sugar
4 eggs
225g (8 oz) baking margarine or butter,
    at room temperature
2 teaspoons baking powder
finely grated zest of 2 lemons

finely grated zest of 2 limes
2 tablespoons milk

TOPPING
175g (6 oz) granulated sugar
juice of 2 limes and 1 lemon

Line a 30 × 23cm (12 × 9 in) traybake tin with foil, and grease well. Preheat the oven to 180°C/350°F/Gas 4.

1 Measure all of the cake ingredients into a large bowl and mix well, using an electric beater.

2 Spoon into the prepared tin and gently level the top. Bake in the preheated oven for 30–35 minutes or until well risen and pale golden brown.

3 Mix together the sugar and lime and lemon juices for the topping and pour over the warm cake. Allow to cool before cutting into squares.

cook now, eat later

TO PREPARE AND COOK AHEAD Bake and complete the cake and store, iced or un-iced, in an airtight container for 2–3 days.

TO FREEZE Leave whole. Pack and freeze, iced or un-iced, for up to 2 months. Thaw at room temperature for 2–3 hours. Cut into squares to serve.

TO COOK IN THE AGA **2-oven Aga:** Bake on the lowest set of runners in the Roasting Oven and slide the cold sheet on the second set of runners. Bake for about 30–35 minutes until pale golden brown and shrinking away from the sides of the tin.

4-oven Aga: Bake on the grid shelf on the floor of the Baking Oven for 30–35 minutes. After 20 minutes, if the cake is getting too brown, slide the cold shelf on the second set of runners.

Banoffee traybake ᵛ

A variation on a traybake, with a naughty toffee icing. Best eaten at room temperature.

Makes 16 pieces

175g (6 oz) baking margarine or butter, at room temperature

250g (9 oz) caster sugar

3 eggs, beaten

3 ripe bananas, mashed

350g (12 oz) self-raising flour

2 teaspoons baking powder

3 tablespoons milk

TOFFEE TOPPING

50g (2 oz) butter

50g (2 oz) light muscovado sugar

1 × 397g can sweetened condensed milk

Line a 30 × 23cm (12 × 9 in) traybake tin or roasting tin with foil, and grease well. Preheat the oven to 180°C/350°F/Gas 4.

1 Measure all the cake ingredients into a large mixing bowl and, using an electric beater, mix until smooth. Spoon into the lined tin and gently level the top. Bake in the oven for about 40–45 minutes or until well risen and golden. Cool in the tin.

2 For the topping, measure the butter, sugar and condensed milk into a saucepan and heat gently until the sugar has dissolved.

3 Bring up to the boil stirring continuously, and simmer for a few minutes until smooth and starting to thicken. Take off the heat and cool slightly, then pour over the cool cake. Spread out evenly with a small palette knife. Allow the caramel to set on the cake before cutting into squares with a hot knife.

cook now, eat later

TO PREPARE AND COOK AHEAD Store iced cake in an airtight container for 2–3 days.

TO FREEZE Leave whole. If freezing the cake iced, open-freeze first then wrap and freeze for up to 2 months. Or freeze the un-iced cake. Unwrap the iced cake, then thaw for about 4 hours at room temperature.

TO COOK IN THE AGA **2-oven Aga:** Bake on the lowest set of runners in the Roasting Oven and slide the cold sheet on to the second set of runners. Bake for about 30–35 minutes until pale golden brown and shrinking away from the sides of the tin.

4-oven Aga: Bake on the grid shelf on the floor of the Baking Oven for about 30–35 minutes. After 20 minutes, if the cake is getting too brown, slide the cold shelf on to the second set of runners.

Apricot and brandy cake V

A beautifully moist, rich cake: ice it for Christmas, or serve plain at any time of year. Make the cake at least 2 weeks ahead so that it is not crumbly. You can feed it with more brandy if you like once it is cooked. Just turn the cake upside down and spoon over a few tablespoons of brandy.

We've also tried this in a 23cm (9 in) round cake tin. It makes a shallower cake, taking about 4¼–4½ hours' cooking time.

Makes 1 × 20cm (8 in) cake

225g (8 oz) ready-to-eat dried apricots, chopped
90ml (3½ fl oz) brandy
225g (8 oz) butter, at room temperature
225g (8 oz) light muscovado sugar
225g (8 oz) plain flour
5 eggs
225g (8 oz) currants

450g (1 lb) sultanas
350g (12 oz) glacé cherries, rinsed, dried and quartered

TO DECORATE
apricot jam for glaze
ready-to-eat dried apricots and glacé fruits

1 Soak the chopped apricots in the brandy overnight.

Grease and line a 20cm (8 in) deep round cake tin with a double layer of greased greaseproof paper. Preheat the oven to 140°C/275°F/Gas 1.

2 Cream the butter and sugar together in a very large mixing bowl, then add the remaining ingredients and continue to mix until well blended.

3 Spoon the mixture into the prepared tin and spread out evenly with the back of a spoon. Cover the top of the cake loosely with a double layer of greaseproof paper.

4 Bake in the preheated oven for about 5 hours or until the cake is a pale golden colour, feels firm to the touch and a skewer inserted into the centre comes out clean. Allow the cake to cool in the tin.

5 Turn out the cake. Glaze with apricot jam. Slice whole apricots in half horizontally and cut any large glacé fruits into slivers if rather thick. Arrange in groups over the top of the cake and glaze again.

recipe continued overleaf

cook now, eat later

TO PREPARE AND COOK AHEAD This cake keeps well as it is so moist. Bake, then cool completely, wrap in the lining paper and foil, and store in a cool place for up to 3 months.

TO FREEZE You may like to freeze the cake if you have made it well ahead and your kitchen is warm. Wrap the cake in clingfilm, put into a large freezer bag and freeze for up to 3 months. To thaw, remove the wrappings and thaw for about 8 hours at room temperature.

TO COOK IN THE AGA Cook on the grid shelf on the floor of the Simmering Oven for 5–15 hours. Simmering Ovens do vary so, hence the time difference. If your Aga is old and the Simmering Oven exceedingly cool, start the cake off in the Roasting Oven on the grid shelf on the floor with the plain shelf above on the second set of runners. Allow to become pale golden then carefully transfer to the Simmering Oven until a skewer comes out clean when inserted in the centre.

Chocolate and rum cake ^V

A very moist cake. This recipe was the one chosen for the chocolate cake competition at our local village show. I was the judge and thought it was delicious. All 12 entries were beautiful, which means it is a sound simple recipe. I've added some rum to the icing, but you could add brandy instead.

Makes 1 × 20cm (8 in) cake

50g (2 oz) cocoa powder	ICING
200ml (7 fl oz) boiling water	100g (4 oz) butter, softened
175g (6 oz) self-raising flour	225g (8 oz) icing sugar
1 rounded teaspoon baking powder	2 dessertspoons cocoa powder
100g (4 oz) butter, softened	2 tablespoons rum or brandy (or water)
275g (10 oz) caster sugar	
2 eggs	

Grease and base-line two 20cm (8 in) deep sandwich tins. Preheat the oven to 180°C/350°F/Gas 4.

1 In a large bowl whisk the cocoa powder with the boiling water, adding it slowly at first, until a smooth consistency. Add the remaining ingredients, and blend together using an electric hand whisk.

2 Divide the mixture between the tins and bake in the middle of the oven for about 30–35 minutes or until the cakes start to shrink away from the sides of the tins. Loosen from the tins and cool on a wire rack.

3 For the icing, beat the soft butter until very soft, then add the icing sugar and cocoa powder with the rum, brandy or water. Mix until smooth then sandwich the cakes together with one-third of the icing. Use the remaining icing to cover the top and sides of the cake.

cook now, eat later

TO PREPARE AND COOK AHEAD Store the completed iced cake in an airtight container for up to a week.

TO FREEZE Freeze the completed iced cake in a round plastic freezer container for up to 1 month. Thaw for about 4 hours at room temperature.

TO COOK IN THE AGA **2-oven Aga:** Slide the tins on to the grid shelf on the floor of the Roasting Oven with the cold sheet on the second set of runners for about 20–25 minutes, turning once half-way through, until the cakes are shrinking away from the sides of the tins.

4-oven Aga: Bake on the grid shelf on the floor of the Baking Oven for about 20–25 minutes.

Apricot and walnut breakfast muffins ∨

Don't expect these to be very sweet; they are more like traditional American muffins. They're perfect for breakfast served warm, and are delicious with honey.

Makes 12

275g (10 oz) self-raising flour
1 level teaspoon baking powder
2 eggs
75g (3 oz) caster sugar
225ml (8 fl oz) milk
100g (4 oz) butter, melted and
   cooled slightly

1 teaspoon vanilla extract
175g (6 oz) ready-to-eat dried apricots,
   snipped into small pieces
50g (2 oz) shelled walnuts,
   roughly chopped

Arrange 12 paper muffin cases in a muffin tin if you have one, or on a baking sheet. Preheat the oven to 200°C/400°F/Gas 6.

1 Measure all the ingredients into a bowl and beat well to mix. Divide the mixture between the paper muffin cases.

2 Bake in the middle of the preheated oven for about 25–30 minutes or until well risen, cooked through and golden. Remove to a wire rack to cool.

cook now, eat later

TO PREPARE AND COOK AHEAD Best eaten freshly made, but can be baked 2 days ahead and refreshed in a moderate oven at 180°C/350°F/Gas 4 for 10 minutes.

TO FREEZE Cool, pack and freeze for up to 4 months. Thaw at room temperature for about 2 hours. Refresh in the oven as above to serve.

TO COOK IN THE AGA Bake on the grid shelf on the floor of the Roasting Oven for about 10–15 minutes until golden brown and well risen, then slide the cold shelf on to the second set of runners for a further 10 minutes or until cooked through.

Sultana spice traybake ^V

This recipe is egg free, therefore the texture is not as light as that of some traybakes. It is quite a thick mixture when it goes into the tin. It is fairly plain so is ideal to have for elevenses.

Makes 16 pieces

500g (1 lb 2 oz) self-raising flour	175g (6 oz) caster sugar
275g (10 oz) baking margarine or butter,	175g (6 oz) sultanas
at room temperature	grated zest of 1 orange
2 level teaspoons baking powder	300ml (½ pint) milk
1 teaspoon mixed spice	demerara sugar

Preheat the oven to 200°C/400°F/Gas 6. Base-line a 30 × 23cm (9 × 12 in) traybake tin or roasting tin with greased baking paper.

1 Measure all the ingredients, except the milk and demerara sugar, into a bowl, and mix with an electric hand whisk, or by hand, until evenly blended. Gradually add the milk, stirring all the time, until well incorporated.

2 Spoon into the lined tin and level out, then sprinkle generously with demerara sugar. Bake in the preheated oven for about 30–35 minutes until golden brown and firm to the touch. Allow to cool in the tin before turning out.

cook now, eat later

TO PREPARE AND COOK AHEAD This can be made a couple of days in advance, but is best eaten as fresh as possible.

TO FREEZE Bake the traybake and cool. Wrap and freeze for up to 3 months. Thaw at room temperature for about 3–4 hours.

TO COOK IN THE AGA 2-oven Aga: Bake on the grid shelf on the floor of the Roasting Oven with the cold sheet on the second set of runners for about 20–25 minutes until golden brown and firm to the touch.

4-oven Aga: Bake on the grid shelf on the floor of the Baking Oven for about 20–25 minutes. If getting too brown, slide the cold shelf above on the second set of runners.

Orange chocolate shortbread biscuits ^V

A variation on an old classic, and very easy to make. The chocolate becomes crisp and crunchy.

Makes 20 biscuits

175g (6 oz) butter, softened	75g (3 oz) cornflour or semolina
75g (3 oz) caster sugar	1 × 85g bar Terry's chocolate orange,
175g (6 oz) plain flour	chopped into small pieces

Preheat the oven to 190°C/375°F/Gas 5. Lightly grease two baking trays.

1 Measure the butter and sugar into a food processor and process until soft. Add the flour and cornflour or semolina and process until beginning to form coarse breadcrumbs. Scrape down the sides, remove the blade and stir in the chocolate pieces.

2 Shape the mixture into 20 even-sized balls and put on to the prepared baking trays. Flatten each ball with a fork. Bake in the preheated oven for about 15–20 minutes until the edges of the biscuits are golden. Allow to cool for a few minutes then transfer to a wire rack until cold.

cook now, eat later

TO PREPARE AND COOK AHEAD Bake, cool and store the biscuits in an airtight container for up to 1 week.

TO FREEZE Pack the cooked biscuits into a rigid freezer-proof container and freeze for up to 2 months. Thaw at room temperature for 1–2 hours.

TO COOK IN THE AGA 2-oven Aga: Place the baking sheet on the floor of the Roasting Oven for about 4 minutes. Take out of the oven, put the grid shelf on the floor and return the biscuits to the grid shelf. Cook for a further 4 minutes until just pale golden at the edges. Do watch very carefully, if necessary sliding the cold sheet on the second set of runners above the biscuits to prevent further browning. Transfer to the Simmering Oven for a further 30–35 minutes until the biscuits are cooked through.

4-oven Aga: Bake on the floor of the Baking Oven for 5 minutes. Take out of the oven, put the grid shelf on the floor and return the biscuits to the grid shelf. Cook for a further 10 minutes until just pale golden at the edges. Watch carefully, if necessary sliding the cold sheet on the second set of runners above the biscuits to prevent further browning. Transfer to the Simmering Oven for a further 30–35 minutes until the biscuits are cooked through.

Clockwise from left: Mega Chocolate Cookies; Frangipane Mince Pies; Orange Chocolate Shortbread Biscuits

Fresh raspberry scones ^V

Fresh blueberries can replace the raspberries if wished, but we prefer the raspberries! The scone dough is very deep to cut out once layered with the raspberries, so flour the cutter well between each cutting to prevent the dough sticking.

The large scone made from the trimmings is perfect sliced for the family.

Makes about 12 small scones

450g (1 lb) self-raising flour	2 eggs
4 teaspoons baking powder	milk
100g (4 oz) butter, softened	about 100g (4 oz) fresh raspberries
50g (2 oz) caster sugar	

Lightly grease 2 baking trays. Preheat the oven to 220°C/425°F/Gas 7.

1 Measure the flour and baking powder into a large bowl. Add the butter and rub in with the fingertips until the mixture resembles fine breadcrumbs. Stir in the sugar.

2 Break the eggs into a measuring jug, then make up to 300ml (½ pint) with milk. Stir the egg and milk mixture into the flour – you may not need it all – and mix to a soft but not sticky dough.

3 Turn out on to a lightly floured work surface, knead lightly and then roll out to a rectangle about 2cm (¾ in) thick. Cut the rectangle of dough into 2 equal pieces.

4 Scatter the fresh raspberries evenly over 1 piece of dough. Top with the second rectangle of dough. Cut into as many rounds as possible with a fluted 5cm (2 in) cutter, and place them on the prepared baking trays. Gently push the trimmings together to form 1 large scone, and score the top with a sharp knife. Brush the tops of the scones with a little extra milk, or any egg and milk left in the jug.

5 Bake in the preheated oven for about 15 minutes or until the scones are well risen and a pale golden brown. (The large scone will need about a further 5 minutes.) Lift on to a wire rack to cool. Eat as fresh as possible.

cook now, eat later

TO PREPARE AND COOK AHEAD Best eaten on the day of making. If you must, store in the fridge for 1 day once cooked. To serve, refresh in a preheated oven at 180°C/350°F/Gas 4 for about 10 minutes.

TO FREEZE These freeze extremely well. Freeze the cooled scones in plastic bags for up to 6 months. Thaw in the plastic bags for 2–3 hours at room temperature, and reheat to serve as above.

TO COOK IN THE AGA Cook on the grid shelf on the lowest set of runners of the Roasting Oven for about 10–15 minutes.

Mega chocolate cookies ᵛ

For speed you can use chocolate chips/polka dots, but we like the large chunks of roughly chopped chocolate! Of course you can make normal-sized biscuits from the same mixture.

Makes 16

225g (8 oz) butter, softened	2 eggs, beaten
175g (6 oz) caster sugar	300g (11 oz) self-raising flour
100g (4 oz) light muscovado sugar	225g (8 oz) plain chocolate, cut into
1 teaspoon vanilla extract	chunky pieces

Lightly grease four baking trays. Preheat the oven to 190°C/375°F/Gas 5.

1 Measure the butter and sugars into a large bowl and mix thoroughly until evenly blended. Add the vanilla extract to the eggs, then add these gradually to the mixture in the bowl, beating well between each addition. Next add the flour, mix in and lastly stir in the chocolate chunks.

2 Spoon large tablespoons of the mixture on to the prepared baking trays, leaving room for the cookies to spread. (You will only be able to fit about 4 per tray!)

3 Bake in the top of the oven for about 15 minutes or until the cookies are just golden. Allow the cookies to cool on the tray for a couple of minutes before lifting off with a palette knife or fish slice. Allow to cool completely on a wire rack.

cook now, eat later

TO PREPARE AND COOK AHEAD Make up to 2 days ahead, store in an airtight container and refresh in a moderate oven at 180°C/350°F/Gas 4 for 8–10 minutes. Cool to let them become crisp, and serve.

TO FREEZE Cool the cookies completely. Pack and freeze for up to 2 months. Thaw at room temperature for 1–2 hours. Refresh in a warm oven. Cool to let them become crisp, then serve.

TO COOK IN THE AGA **2-oven Aga:** Cook on the grid shelf on the floor of the Roasting Oven with the cold shelf on the second set of runners for about 15–20 minutes, turning round after about 10 minutes. In the Aga the cookies will spread slightly more than in a conventional oven.

4-oven Aga: Cook on the grid shelf on the floor of the Baking Oven with the cold sheet on the second set of runners for about 15–20 minutes. If not quite brown enough, remove the cold sheet for the final 5 minutes.

Apple and lemon drop scones ^V

Drop scones and Scotch pancakes are the same thing. It's essential to make them and eat them straightaway whilst still warm, with butter or lemon curd.

Makes 10–12 scones

100g (4 oz) plain flour
1½ teaspoons baking powder
25g (1 oz) caster sugar
finely grated zest of 1 lemon, plus 1
  teaspoon lemon juice
25g (1 oz) butter, melted

1 egg
100ml (4 fl oz) milk
1 small Cox's apple, peeled
vegetable oil or white vegetable fat for
  greasing

1 Measure the flour, baking powder, sugar and lemon zest into a bowl and mix lightly. Make a well in the centre then mix in the butter, egg, milk and lemon juice. Gradually draw the dry ingredients into the liquid to make a smooth thick batter. Coarsely grate in the apple.

2 Prepare a griddle or heavy-based frying pan (preferably non-stick) by heating and greasing with oil or white vegetable fat.

3 Drop the mixture in spoonfuls on to the hot griddle, spacing the mixture well apart. When bubbles rise to the surface, turn the scones over with a palette knife and cook them on the other side for a further 30 seconds to 1 minute until they are golden brown. Continue cooking until all of the mixture has been used.

4 Lift off on to a wire rack and cover them with a clean tea-towel to keep them soft. Serve warm.

cook now, eat later

TO PREPARE AHEAD The batter can be made the day before, but grate in the apple at the last minute. Best freshly made to order.

TO FREEZE Not suitable as the drop scones go rather rubbery.

TO COOK ON THE AGA Grease the Simmering Plate lightly with a little oil (use a pad of kitchen paper to do this). If your Simmering Plate is particularly hot it may be necessary to lift the lid for a couple of minutes to reduce the heat slightly. Spoon the mixture on to the plate in tablespoons, spacing them well apart (about 4 at a time). When bubbles rise to the surface, turn the drop scones over with a palette knife, and cook on the other side for a further 30 seconds or so until golden brown. Lift off and serve.

CHRISTMAS AT HOME

All my Christmases have been at home in recent years, but I well remember when we used to take everything – the turkey, stuffing, vegetables, all prepared in advance – over to Granny's on Christmas Eve, ready to be cooked the next day. It was all a matter of meticulous organisation, and that still applies today.

Order your turkey or goose well in advance. If choosing a frozen turkey, the fresh frozen are better than the water-cooled. Defrost thoroughly in a cool place – *not* the fridge, and *not* a freezing garage! The stuffings can be made and frozen well ahead, as can things like mince pies, ice-cream and cakes. And of course, if you've made a Christmas pudding yourself, that will be ready several months in advance.

For the day itself, the turkey can be stuffed (breast end only) some hours before cooking, so long as it is in the fridge. Make a stock from the giblets the day before. If making the chestnut stuffing, look out for those wonderful frozen chestnuts, which appear just before Christmas in the best supermarkets. If you can't get hold of them, use the dried, but remember to buy half the weight asked for in the recipe – they plump up after an overnight soak. You could already have breadcrumbs for the stuffing in the freezer, but make sure you have pure white for the bread sauce. You can prepare the vegetables the day before – peeling, trimming and chopping – and if you're offering a root vegetable purée, that could be happily in the fridge awaiting its reheating. Part-roast your potatoes and parsnips ready for a quick blast in the oven once the turkey is resting.

The recipes here are traditional, but most have a twist, something you might like to try – and that your family might appreciate – just as a change on Christmas Day. The puddings in particular are different. You could try the ice-cream instead of brandy butter with your Christmas pudding (and it could be made with rum instead). All can be prepared ahead, making for a relaxed and enjoyable day for all – especially the cook!

Traditional Roast Turkey

Scarlet Confit

Apricot and Chestnut Stuffing

Lemon and Thyme Pork Stuffing

Mincemeat Bread and Butter Pudding

Frangipane Mince Pies

Brandy Ice-cream

Classic Victorian Christmas Cake

Christmas Chocolate Log

Apple Mincemeat Alaska

For more Christmas ideas, see:

Spicy Turkey Fajitas (see page 140)

Turkey Salad with Avocado, Bacon and Pesto Dressing (see page 141)

Glazed Apple Gammon (see page 189)

Cockatrice (see page 196)

Apricot and Brandy Cake (see page 210)

Traditional roast turkey

I use a meat thermometer when cooking turkey – it helps to judge when the turkey is done. Cook it to 75°–80°C rather than the 90°C suggested on the thermometer gauge.

Serves about 20

1 × 7.5kg (17 lb) oven-ready turkey	sprigs of fresh thyme
butter, softened	onion
lemon, thinly sliced	

Preheat the oven to 220°C/425°F/Gas 7.

1 Loosen the skin over the breast of the turkey by slipping your fingers between the flesh and skin, leaving the skin attached at the neck end. Spread softened butter over the top of the breast under the skin, holding the skin up. Slip in lemon slices and thyme, under the skin.

2 Stuff the breast end of the turkey with *Lemon and Thyme Pork Stuffing* (see page 229). Secure the loose skin with fine skewers. Fill the body cavity with any lemon trimmings, herbs and large pieces of onion. Tie the legs with string to give a neat shape. Lightly butter the skin of the bird.

3 Weigh the turkey and calculate the cooking time, allowing 15 minutes per 450g (1 lb). Arrange 2 large sheets of foil across a large roasting tin. Place the turkey on top and insert a meat thermometer into the thickest part of the thigh. (When cooked it will register 75°–80°C.) Fold the sheets of foil loosely over the turkey, leaving a large air gap between the turkey and the foil.

4 Cook the turkey in the preheated oven for about 30 minutes. Reduce the oven temperature to 160°C/325°F/Gas 3 and cook for 30 minutes short of the cooking time, basting from time to time.

5 Remove the foil 30 minutes before the end of cooking time and increase heat to 220°C/425°F/Gas 7 to crisp the skin.

6 If not using a thermometer, pierce the thickest part of the thigh with a small sharp knife. If the juices are clear, then the turkey is done; if they are still tinged with pink, then cook for a little longer. Cover turkey and leave to stand for 30 minutes before carving.

7 Drain off the liquid from the tin, skim off the fat and keep the stock for gravy.

8 Serve with bacon rolls, gravy, sausages, bread sauce, *Scarlet Confit* (see page 227) and *Apricot and Chestnut Stuffing* (see page 228).

recipe continued overleaf

cook now, eat later

TO PREPARE AHEAD Prepare to the end of step 3 up to 12 hours before. Cover and chill until ready to cook.

TO FREEZE The raw stuffings can be frozen for up to 1 month in advance.

TO COOK IN THE AGA Slow roasting: Place on the grid shelf on the floor of the Simmering Oven. If the turkey is over 8.1kg (18 lb), or if your Simmering Oven is on the cool side, start off in the Roasting Oven uncovered for 30 minutes, then cover with foil and transfer to the Simmering Oven (see chart below).

3.6–4.5kg (8–10 lb) turkey, about 10 hours

5–7.25kg (11–16 lb) turkey, about 12 hours (overnight)

7.5–10kg (17–22 lb) turkey, about 14 hours (overnight)

To brown, when the bird is done, put uncovered into the Roasting Oven for about 15 minutes.

Fast roasting: Cook in the roasting tin lightly covered with foil on the grid shelf on the floor of the Roasting Oven.

3.6–4.5kg (8–10 lb) turkey, about 1¾–2 hours

5–7.25kg (11–16 lb) turkey, about 2½ hours

7.5–10kg (17–22 lb) turkey, about 3 hours

Baste the bird from time to time. Remove the foil 30 minutes before the end of cooking time to crisp the skin.

TIP Do not put a meat stuffing into the cavity of a bird as this is not safe. Put in only flavouring, vegetables and herbs.

Scarlet confit

Gently reheat to serve with hot game casseroles and roast turkey or game birds.

Serves 20

450g (1 lb) fresh or frozen cranberries
225g (8 oz) granulated sugar
finely grated zest and juice of 1 orange
50ml (2 fl oz) port

50ml (2 fl oz) cider vinegar
a large pinch of ground allspice
a large pinch of ground cinnamon

1 Measure all the ingredients into a shallow pan.

2 Bring to the boil and simmer gently for about 10–15 minutes, stirring from time to time. Don't worry if it looks a bit runny as it thickens when it cools.

cook now, eat later

TO PREPARE AND COOK AHEAD Cook and keep covered in the fridge for up to 1 month.

TO FREEZE Cool quickly, pack and freeze for up to 3 months. Leave at room temperature to defrost.

TO COOK IN THE AGA Cook uncovered in the Simmering Oven for about 1 hour.

Apricot and chestnut stuffing

A really good stuffing to serve with turkey, chicken or goose.

Serves 6

225g (8 oz) ready-to-eat dried apricots
600ml (1 pint) water
1 large onion, coarsely chopped
225g (8 oz) white breadcrumbs
75g (3 oz) butter

225g (8 oz) frozen chestnuts, thawed
and roughly chopped
a generous bunch of fresh parsley,
chopped
salt and freshly ground black pepper

You will need a shallow ovenproof dish, about 20 × 28 × 5cm (8 × 11 × 2 in).

Preheat the oven to 190°C/375°F/Gas 5.

1 Chop the apricots into small pieces, the size of raisins.

2 Measure the water into a pan, add the onion and apricot pieces, and boil for 5 minutes. Drain well.

3 Put the breadcrumbs into a large bowl. Melt the butter in a pan and pour half of it on to the breadcrumbs.

4 Add the chestnuts to the remaining melted butter and brown lightly. Mix together with the apricots, onion, parsley and breadcrumbs. Season well and taste.

5 Turn into a buttered, ovenproof dish and bake for about 25–30 minutes until crisp.

cook now, eat later

TO PREPARE AND COOK AHEAD Prepare to the end of step 4. Cover and keep in the fridge for up to 1 day before cooking. Cook as above but for a little longer.

TO FREEZE Freeze at the end of step 4 for about 1 month. Defrost and reheat to serve as above until piping hot.

TO COOK IN THE AGA Slide the dish on to the floor of the Roasting Oven for about 25–30 minutes until crisp.

Lemon and thyme pork stuffing

This is a favourite family recipe, served for every Christmas as long as I can remember! This is the stuffing for the breast end of the turkey: do not put a meat stuffing in the body cavity of a bird.

Sufficient to stuff a 7.2–8.1 (16–18 lb) turkey in the breast end

40g (1½ oz) butter

1 large onion, chopped

700g (1½ lb) pork sausagemeat

150g (5 oz) fresh white breadcrumbs

finely grated zest and juice of

  1 large lemon

salt and freshly ground black pepper

3 tablespoons chopped fresh parsley

leaves from 6 sprigs of fresh thyme,

  or 1 level teaspoon dried thyme

1 Melt the butter in a saucepan, add the onion and cook gently until soft, about 10 minutes.

2 Stir in the remaining ingredients and mix well together.

cook now, eat later

TO PREPARE AND COOK AHEAD Make the day before, cover and keep in the fridge.

TO FREEZE The stuffing can be made and frozen for up to 3 months so long as the pork sausagemeat has not been previously frozen. Leave at room temperature to defrost.

TO COOK IN THE AGA Cook the onion in the Simmering Oven until soft.

Mincemeat bread and butter pudding

This is wonderful at any time of the year, not just at Christmas! It is essential to make it in a shallow dish so that you get maximum crunchy top. It rises like a soufflé, so serve at once straight from the oven.

Serves 6–8

50g (2 oz) ready-to-eat dried apricots	3 large eggs
2 tablespoons brandy or rum	150ml (¼ pint) double cream
12 thin slices white bread, buttered	1 teaspoon vanilla extract
1 × 450g jar luxury mincemeat	300ml (½ pint) milk
50g (2 oz) caster sugar	1 tablespoon demerara sugar

Well butter a 28cm (11 in) fairly shallow, round, china ovenproof dish. Preheat the oven to 180°C/350°F/Gas 4.

1 Snip the apricots into smallish pieces and soak in the brandy or rum whilst making the pudding.

2 Make sandwiches of the bread using the mincemeat, but don't fill right to the edges because they are trimmed off. Cut off the crusts and cut each sandwich diagonally into four. Arrange the sandwich triangles across the dish, slightly overlapping.

3 Beat together the caster sugar, eggs, cream and vanilla extract. Stir in the milk.

4 Scatter the apricots over the bread. Gradually pour over the cream mixture, making sure all the bread is coated. Leave the pudding to stand for 30–60 minutes. (This allows the bread to absorb the liquid so it becomes light and crisp during cooking.)

5 Sprinkle the demerara sugar over the top of the pudding, and bake in the preheated oven for about 40 minutes until well risen, crisp and golden. Serve warm with crème fraîche or cream.

cook now, eat later

TO PREPARE AHEAD Complete to the end of step 4 up to 12 hours ahead, cover with clingfilm and leave in the fridge. Continue with step 5.

TO FREEZE Not suitable.

TO COOK IN THE AGA Bake on the grid shelf on the floor of the Roasting Oven, with the cold sheet on the second set of runners, for about 25 minutes.

Frangipane mince pies

A new variation on an old favourite. If you want to make a large tart you can use the exact quantity below to fill a 23cm (9 in) loose-bottomed flan tin which will take about 25 minutes in the preheated oven.

Makes 24

PASTRY
225g (8 oz) plain flour
100g (4 oz) butter, cut into cubes
25g (1 oz) icing sugar
1 egg, beaten

FRANGIPANE
100g (4 oz) softened butter
100g (4 oz) caster sugar
2 large eggs
100g (4 oz) ground almonds

15g (½ oz) plain flour
½ teaspoon almond extract, or to taste

FILLING AND TOPPING
just under 1 × 410g jar mincemeat
    flavoured with about 2 tablespoons
    brandy
a few flaked almonds
apricot jam to glaze

You will need deep mince pie tins for 24 pies and a 6.5cm (2½ in) cutter.

Preheat the oven to 200°C/400°F/Gas 6.

1 To make the pastry, measure the flour, butter and icing sugar into a food processor bowl, then process until the mixture resembles breadcrumbs. Pour in the beaten egg and pulse the blade until the dough starts to form a ball. Knead lightly, wrap and chill for about 30 minutes.

2 To make the frangipane, measure the butter and sugar into the unwashed processor, and blend until soft and creamy. Scrape down the sides, add the eggs and continue to process. Don't worry if the mixture looks curdled at this stage. Add the ground almonds, flour and almond extract, and mix briefly.

3 Roll the pastry out thinly on a lightly floured work surface and line the tins. Spoon a teaspoon of mincemeat into each tartlet and top with the frangipane mixture. There is no need to spread the mixture flat as it will level out in the oven (but do not over-fill the tins). Sprinkle a few flaked almonds on top.

4 Bake in the preheated oven for about 15–17 minutes, watching carefully. Remove from the tins and allow to cool a little on a wire rack.

5 Dilute the apricot jam with a little lemon juice or water and bring to the boil. Brush each warm tartlet with glaze. Like traditional mince pies, these are best served warm.

cook now, eat later

TO PREPARE AND COOK AHEAD Complete to the end of step 5 up to 3 days ahead. Refresh in a moderate oven at 180°C/350°F/Gas 4 for about 8–10 minutes.

TO FREEZE Freeze the mince pies at the end of step 5. Thaw at room temperature for 2–3 hours. Warm through in the oven as above.

TO COOK IN THE AGA Bake directly on the floor of the Roasting Oven for about 8 minutes to brown the pastry base. Turn round and slide on the grid shelf on the floor of the Roasting Oven for a further 6–8 minutes until well risen and golden brown. You may need the cold sheet on the second set of runners if getting too brown.

Brandy ice-cream

This ice-cream does not need a second whisking so is very quick and easy, and is very good with Christmas pudding, mince pies and tarts. It contains raw egg yolks so is not suitable for pregnant ladies or the very young or elderly.

Serves 8

4 eggs, separated	300ml (½ pint) double cream
100g (4 oz) caster sugar	2 tablespoons brandy

1 Whisk the egg whites on fast speed, using an electric hand whisk, until light and stiff. Beat in the sugar, still on a fast speed, a little at a time until a thick glossy meringue. Fold in the egg yolks.

2 Whisk the cream and brandy together until thick. Fold into the meringue mixture.

3 Freeze in a flat polythene box overnight, for at least 12 hours.

cook now, eat later

TO PREPARE AHEAD AND FREEZE Freeze for up to 1 month.

Classic Victorian Christmas cake

Remember to make time, some 3 days, for marinating the fruit in sherry. This is essential to plump up and flavour the fruit. If you cut the soaking time, there will be surplus liquid which will alter the texture of the cake. You should make this cake at least 3 weeks ahead of Christmas, for if eaten too early it is crumbly. This is not a very deep cake.

Makes 1 × 23cm (9 in) cake

175g (6 oz) raisins
350g (12 oz) glacé cherries, rinsed and
  dried thoroughly
500g (1 lb 2 oz) currants
350g (12 oz) sultanas
150ml (¼ pint) sherry
finely grated zest of 2 oranges
250g (9 oz) softened butter
250g (9 oz) light muscovado sugar
4 eggs
1 tablespoon black treacle

75g (3 oz) blanched almonds, chopped
75g (3 oz) self-raising flour
175g (6 oz) plain flour
1½ teaspoons mixed ground spice

TO FINISH AND DECORATE
medium sherry
apricot jam
glacé fruits
nuts

1 First prepare the fruit: chop the raisins with a damp knife and quarter the cherries. Put all the fruit in a container, pour over the sherry and stir in the orange zest. Cover with a lid and leave to soak for 3 days, stirring daily.

Grease and line a 23cm (9 in) deep round tin with greased greaseproof paper. Preheat the oven to 140°C/275°F/Gas 1.

2 Measure the butter, sugar, eggs, treacle and almonds into a large bowl and beat well. Add the flours and spice and mix thoroughly until blended. Stir in the soaked fruit. Spoon into the prepared cake tin and level the surface. Cover the top of the cake loosely with a double layer of greaseproof paper.

3 Bake in the centre of the preheated oven for about 5–5½ hours or until the cake feels firm to the touch and is a rich golden brown. A skewer inserted into the centre of the cake should come out clean. Leave the cake to cool in the tin.

4 When cool, pierce the cake at intervals with a fine skewer and feed with a little sherry. Wrap the completely cold cake in a double layer of greaseproof paper and again in foil and store in a cool place for up to 3 months, feeding at intervals with more sherry. (Don't remove the lining paper when storing as this helps to keep the cake moist.)

5 To decorate, brush sieved, warmed apricot jam over the top of the cake. Arrange glacé fruits and nuts over the jam and brush again with jam.

cook now, eat later

TO PREPARE AND COOK AHEAD Prepare the fruit and soak in sherry 3 days ahead. Make the cake and wrap as in step 4. Store in a cool place for up to 3 months, following step 4.

TO FREEZE Freeze for up to 3 months, then defrost at room temperature.

TO COOK IN THE AGA Baking the cake slowly in the Simmering Oven gives excellent results. Don't bake overnight, as it could be overbaked. I find it best to mix the cake and put it into the tin the day before, then bake it starting first thing in the morning in the Simmering Oven. Choose a day when you are at home and can keep an eye on it. In my Aga it takes 5½ hours. In a converted Aga or old Aga with a slower Simmering Oven, I find it best to start it off in the Roasting Oven on the grid shelf on the floor with the cold shelf on the second set of runners for about 30 minutes or until just pale golden, then transfer to the Simmering Oven until done. Consult your original Aga book.

Christmas chocolate log

An easy Yule log, with a delicious filling and icing. The apricot jam helps the icing to stick to the cake, and is delicious too. You don't need to wait until Christmas, though the cake can be made at any time of the year for a special occasion.

Serves 10–12

CHOCOLATE SPONGE	CHOCOLATE ICING AND TOPPING
4 large eggs	275g (10 oz) Bournville chocolate, in
100g (4 oz) caster sugar	small pieces
65g (2½ oz) self-raising flour	450ml (¾ pint) double cream
40g (1½ oz) cocoa powder	4 tablespoons apricot jam
	icing sugar for dusting

Preheat the oven to 200°C/400°F/Gas 6. Grease and line a 33 × 23cm (13 × 9 in) Swiss roll tin with non-stick paper, securing the corners with metal paperclips.

1 For the sponge, whisk the eggs and sugar using an electric hand whisk in a large bowl until the mixture is pale in colour, light and frothy. Sift the flour and cocoa powder into the bowl and carefully cut and fold together, using a metal spoon, until all the cocoa and flour is incorporated into the egg mixture. (Be careful not to beat any of the air out of the mixture.)

2 Pour into the lined tin and spread out into the corners. Bake in the middle of the preheated oven for about 8–10 minutes until pale golden and the sides are shrinking away from the edge of the tin.

3 Place a piece of greaseproof paper bigger than the Swiss roll on the work surface. Invert the cake on to the paper and remove (and count!) the paperclips and bottom lining piece of paper.

4 Trim the edges of the cake with a sharp knife and make a score mark 2.5cm (1 in) in along the longer edge. Roll up (from the longer edge) using the paper, rolling with the paper inside. Set aside to cool.

5 While the cake is cooling, make the icing. Melt the chocolate and 300ml (½ pint) of the cream in a bowl over a pan of simmering water until completely melted (be careful not to overheat). Put into the fridge to cool and firm up (this icing needs to be very thick for piping). Whip the remaining cream.

recipe continued overleaf

6 Uncurl the cold Swiss roll and remove the paper. Spread a third of the icing over the surface then spread the whipped cream on top, and re-roll tightly. Cut a quarter of the cake off from one end on the diagonal. Transfer the large piece of cake to a serving plate and angle the cut end to the side of the large cake to make a branch. Cover the surface of the cake with the melted apricot jam.

7 Put the remaining chocolate icing into a piping bag fitted with a star nozzle. Pipe long thick lines along the cake, covering the cake completely so it looks like the bark of a tree. Cover each end with icing or, if you wish to see the cream, leave un-iced.

8 Dust with icing sugar and garnish with fresh holly to serve.

cook now, eat later

TO PREPARE AND COOK AHEAD Make completely, filled and iced, up to 2 days ahead. If there is time, though, it is best made on the day of serving.

TO FREEZE Freezes well filled, iced, or un-iced for up to 1 month. Ideally it should be frozen filled and rolled but un-iced, then iced once defrosted, which ensures the icing keeps a nice shine. Defrost in the fridge overnight to serve.

TO COOK IN THE AGA Cook the cake on the grid shelf on the floor of the Roasting Oven for about 8–10 minutes or until shrinking away from the sides of the tin. You may need to slide in the cold sheet on the second set of runners if getting too brown. Follow the rest of the recipe as above.

Make the icing by breaking the chocolate into a large bowl with 300ml (½ pint) of the cream and putting into the Simmering Oven for about 20 minutes or until melted, stirring occasionally.

Apple mincemeat Alaska

This is a very quick and easy pudding, best served warm with cream. Use the spare egg yolks to make fresh lemon curd (see page 170).

Serves 6–8

900g (2 lb) cooking apples, peeled and cored, thickly sliced	4 tablespoons brandy or Calvados
25g (1 oz) butter	MERINGUE
juice and zest of ½ lemon	3 large egg whites
8 trifle sponges, about 175g (6 oz)	175g (6 oz) caster sugar
1 × 400g jar good-quality mincemeat	

Butter a 20–23cm (8–9 in) round, shallow china ovenproof dish. Preheat the oven to 180°C/ 350°F/Gas 4.

1 Thickly slice the apples into a shallow saucepan with the butter, lemon juice and zest. Heat gently until the butter has melted, then cover and simmer gently for about 15–20 minutes until the apples are tender. Allow to cool slightly. Arrange the trifle sponges evenly over the base of the dish, cutting to fit.

2 Whisk the egg whites for the meringue in a large clean bowl with an electric hand whisk on full speed until stiff. Gradually add the sugar, 1 teaspoon at a time, whisking continuously, still on full speed, until the mixture is stiff and glossy.

3 Mix the mincemeat and brandy or Calvados with the apples and spread over the trifle sponges. Spoon the meringue mixture on top and spread out evenly, covering all the mincemeat and apples so no holes appear.

4 Bake in the preheated oven for about 20–25 minutes, watching carefully, until the meringue is crisp and a pale golden brown. Serve immediately.

cook now, eat later

TO PREPARE AHEAD Prepare step 1 up to 6 hours ahead.

TO FREEZE Not suitable.

TO COOK IN THE AGA Bring the apples to heat on the Boiling Plate, then cover and transfer to the Simmering Oven for about 30 minutes until the apples are tender. At step 4, slide the dish on to the grid shelf on the floor of the Roasting Oven for about 4 minutes until pale golden brown. Transfer to the Simmering Oven for a further 30 minutes until the meringue is crisp. Serve immediately.

BITS AND BOBS
TO GO WITH DRINKS

Preparing what I call 'bits and bobs' for drinks parties is generally considered to be very labour-intensive. And so it is: everything is smaller, so shaping, cutting and putting toppings and garnishes on bases is much more intricate and detailed. This takes time as well, but all the recipes here can be prepared in advance, so it won't seem too much of a chore. The different stages may have to be brought together and/or cooked at the last minute, but the bulk of the work is out of the way. All you will have to do on the day is make things look pretty on platters.

Dips are very useful, and the two here can be made a bit in advance, and can be used with crudités or spread on crostini or pitta breads. The crostini themselves are a huge life-saver to me: store them in the freezer in plastic boxes with kitchen paper in between the layers. They're immediately to hand, take no time to defrost, and are handy for any topping. The Roquefort and pear crostini were the hit of last Christmas in our household (although I have to admit I used Stilton, as we had so much left over). The smoked salmon canapés may sound fiddly, but they're not at all, due to the crafty way we put them together (and in advance!). But the best canapés of the lot are the soufflé croûtons which are so simple and delicious, and can be baked straight from the freezer.

When planning a drinks party, have it clear in your head – and make it clear to your guests too! – exactly what it is you are offering. What time of day will it be, will people be hungry? You're not meant to be offering them a meal, just something to accompany the drinks. Bite-sized canapés that are full of flavour are the order of the day usually, and I work on about 5 per person. But if you think people might like something more substantial, you could make more canapés in general, or make some of the dishes here a little larger – the toad in the hole, for instance, baked in mince-pie tins.

Tiny New Potatoes with Dill Herrings

Roquefort and Pear Crostini **V**

Sweet Pepper and Herb Dip **V**

Scrumptious Smoked Salmon Canapés

Miniature Bangers and Mash

Wonderful Soufflé Croûtons **V**

Mustard and Parmesan Cheese Straws **V**

Cocktail Toad in the Hole

Home-made Garlic Herb Cheese **V**

Peppadew and Chèvre Crostini **V**

For more canapé ideas, see:

Garlic-stuffed Grilled Mussels (see page 22)

Crab Cakes with Mild Chilli Sauce (see page 30)

Spinach and Feta Frittata (see page 110)

Bean Bangers (see page 111)

Herb Falafels (see page 119)

Onion, Apple and Stilton Little Quiches (see page 120)

Frangipane Mince Pies (see page 232)

Tiny new potatoes with dill herrings

An unusual canapé to go with drinks. Buy the smallest new potatoes you can buy. Dill herrings come in a jar (found in the chilled section of any good supermarket with pâtés and smoked salmon) and are very versatile.

Makes 20

10 very small new potatoes, skin on	3 tablespoons crème fraîche
1 × 275g jar herrings in dill marinade	a few sprigs of fresh dill

1 Cook the potatoes in boiling salted water until tender, about 8–10 minutes. Drain, refresh in cold water (to stop the cooking), leave to cool and dry.

2 Slice the potatoes in half lengthways. Slice a very thin layer from the rounded end of each potato half (opposite the sliced side), so they will sit flat on a plate.

3 Drain the herrings from the marinade and slice into 1cm (½ in) pieces (or pieces about half the size of the potato). Spoon a tiny blob of crème fraîche on top of each potato and place a piece of herring on top, with a sprig of dill to garnish.

cook now, eat later

TO PREPARE AND COOK AHEAD These can be completely made up to 12 hours ahead, and kept in the fridge.

TO FREEZE Not suitable.

From back to front: Mustard and Parmesan Cheese Straws;
Wonderful Soufflé Croûtons; Miniature Bangers and Mash;
Tiny New Potatoes with Dill Herrings; Roquefort and Pear Crostini

Roquefort and pear crostini ᵛ

Unusual for a small drinks party, too time-consuming to do for 100! These must be served warm. They even reheat well once made, but they look their best straight from the oven.

Makes 25

1 × 400g can pears	CROSTINI
100g (4 oz) Roquefort cheese	1 small thin, long baguette
paprika	olive oil
chopped fresh chives	salt and freshly ground black pepper

Preheat the grill to the highest setting.

1 First make the crostini. Thinly slice the baguette, brush both sides with oil, season and place on a small baking sheet which will fit under the grill or line the grill pan with foil.

2 To cook the crostini, toast under the grill for about 2–3 minutes each side until pale golden brown and crisp. Watch them carefully. Cool on a wire rack.

3 Drain and slice the pears into thickish pieces about the thickness of a digestive biscuit in a shape just smaller than the crostini.

4 The next process is messy! Either spread a little Roquefort on each crostini then top with pear and spread with a little more Roquefort, or first grate the Roquefort on a coarse grater then spread.

5 When ready to serve, sprinkle with paprika and place under a hot grill for about 4–5 minutes or until the cheese has melted. Sprinkle with chives.

cook now, eat later

TO PREPARE AND COOK AHEAD These can be assembled up to 12 hours ahead. Cover with clingfilm and keep in the fridge until needed. Grill to serve.

TO FREEZE The crostini can be made up to 2 months in advance and frozen. Defrost and assemble with the pears and Roquefort.

TO COOK IN THE AGA For the crostini, arrange them on a baking sheet, cook on the floor of the Roasting Oven, turning once, until golden brown, about 5 minutes. To cook when assembled, slide the baking sheet on the second set of runners in the Roasting Oven for about 4–5 minutes until pale golden and the cheese has melted on the crostini. Watch very carefully. Allow to cool for a moment then scatter with chives and serve.

Sweet pepper and herb dip ^V

A quick and easy dip to make for pitta bread or raw vegetables, and it can also be used as a sauce for a cold cooked chicken salad. Jars of red peppers are available in all good supermarkets or, of course, you could skin a fresh pepper and use that instead. If you do not have a food processor, chop the herbs and red pepper by hand and mix with the other ingredients.

Makes about 600g (1 lb 5 oz)

leaves from a large bunch of fresh parsley
leaves from a large bunch of fresh basil
100g (4 oz) red pepper, from a jar
 (½ x 225g jar)
juice of 1 lemon
1 tablespoon caster sugar
1 x 200g tub full-fat Greek yogurt

200g (7 oz) 'light' low-calorie
 mayonnaise
150g (5 oz) full-fat cream cheese
 (e.g. Philadelphia)
salt and freshly ground black pepper

1 Process the parsley and basil until coarsely chopped in a food processor.

2 Add the red pepper, lemon juice and sugar and whizz for 30 seconds.

3 Add the yogurt, mayonnaise, cream cheese and salt and pepper. Whizz again, check the seasoning and serve.

cook now, eat later

TO PREPARE AHEAD Prepare ahead, and keep covered in the fridge for about 1 week.

TO FREEZE Not suitable.

Scrumptious smoked salmon canapés

This recipe is a wonderful way to make canapés for large numbers of people. It freezes brilliantly in the tin and really is so easy to make – saves all the individual spreading and arranging! Use good-quality slices of smoked salmon for this recipe and not trimmings.

Makes 96

300g (11 oz) full-fat cream cheese	6 slices thinly sliced Hovis bread
finely grated zest of ½ lemon	(large loaf size)
a good handful of fresh dill, chopped	400g (14 oz) smoked salmon slices
salt and freshly ground black pepper	a little black caviar or lumpfish roe
	a few fresh sprigs of dill for garnish

Line a 33 × 23cm (13 × 9 in) Swiss roll tin or flat baking sheet with clingfilm (if you wet the tin first the clingfilm will stick more easily!).

1 Mix the cream cheese, lemon zest and chopped dill together in a bowl and season with salt and pepper. Remove the crusts from the bread and carefully spread each slice with the cream cheese (right into the corners), making sure all the bread is covered.

2 Arrange the bread on the lined tray, cheese side up, so all the sides are touching (3 × 2), and gently spread the cream cheese over the joins, so it looks like one large piece of cheese-covered bread. Slice the smoked salmon into long thin strips and arrange neatly over the cream cheese so all the bread is covered. Cover with clingfilm, and chill for at least 4 hours.

3 Cut into about 96 neat, even-sized squares, and top each square with a tiny blob of caviar or lumpfish roe or a sprig of fresh dill. (It works out at 16 squares per slice of bread, but you can make them larger if you like.)

cook now, eat later

> **TO PREPARE AHEAD AND FREEZE** Freeze the tray after step 2, covered in clingfilm, up to 1 month ahead. Remove from the freezer, leave for about 10 minutes at room temperature, and cut into squares while frozen. Leave to defrost in the fridge, then top with caviar or lumpfish roe and dill.

Miniature bangers and mash

Rather than boiling only 2 small potatoes to fill the sausages, why not boil extra and use the leftovers for supper. Don't forget to warn the guests if the sausages are very hot. When making food for a drinks party, don't forget old favourites like devils-on-horseback (prunes wrapped in bacon). If you haven't already tasted them, cocktail sausages are wonderful served with equal quantities of runny honey and mustard. Coat over the sausages while hot!

Makes 20

20 cocktail pork sausages (Marks & Spencer and some supermarkets sell them ready cooked)	salt and freshly ground black pepper
	grated Parmesan
	paprika
mashed potatoes	

1 Grill the sausages (if raw), turning once or twice until cooked and evenly brown. Allow the sausages to become completely cold as it makes it easier to make a slit down the length to form an opening.

Preheat the oven to 200°C/400°F/Gas 6.

2 Ensure that the potatoes are very well seasoned. Fill into a piping bag fitted with a plain narrow nozzle. (You can also spoon the potato into the sausage.)

3 Hold a sausage, squeezing the ends gently together, and pipe or spoon the potato into the gap.

4 Sprinkle the sausages with Parmesan and dust with paprika. Arrange on a baking tray.

5 Reheat in the preheated oven for about 10 minutes or until piping hot.

cook now, eat later

TO PREPARE AND COOK AHEAD Prepare to the end of step 4 up to 1 day before. Cover and keep in the fridge. Continue with step 5.

TO FREEZE At the end of step 4, pack the sausages in a single layer in a ridged freezer container. Freeze for up to 1 month. Thaw for about 2 hours at room temperature before reheating as in step 5 above.

TO COOK IN THE AGA Cook the sausages on non-stick paper in a roasting tin on the floor of the Roasting Oven until cooked and brown. Reheat in the Roasting Oven on the top set of runners for about 5 minutes.

Wonderful soufflé croûtons V

These are fantastic, so easy to make, and wonderful for nibbles to go with drinks. This batch makes about 100, so great to do for a large number of people. We were given this recipe by one of our Aga enthusiasts who is a caterer and has been to many of our Aga Workshops. We thank her hugely.

Makes about 100

75g (3 oz) full-fat cream cheese	5 × 2.5cm (1 in) slices from a white tin
150g (5 oz) butter	loaf, 2–3 days old, crusts removed
150g (5 oz) Cheddar, grated	salt and freshly ground black pepper
2 large egg whites	

Preheat the oven to 220°C/425°F/Gas 7. Line 2–3 baking sheets with non-stick baking paper or grease lightly.

1 Melt the cream cheese, butter and Cheddar in a pan over a low heat until completely melted (don't worry, the mixture looks very curdled at this stage). Whisk the egg whites until stiff, and fold carefully into the cheese mixture. Season lightly with salt and pepper.

2 Cut each slice of bread into 4 down, 5 across to give 20 × 2.5cm (1 in) cubes for each slice. Dip each cube into the soufflé mixture until completely coated and transfer to the prepared baking sheets.

3 Bake in the preheated oven for about 10 minutes until golden brown and puffed up. Turn over once and check after 6 minutes. Serve at once.

cook now, eat later

TO PREPARE AHEAD AND FREEZE Freeze the raw croûtons at the end of step 2 on the baking sheet for up to 1 month. Remove from the freezer and cook from frozen for about 5 minutes longer than the cooking time above. They freeze brilliantly.

TO COOK IN THE AGA Slide the baking sheet directly on to the floor of the Roasting Oven and bake for about 10–12 minutes, turning the croûtons over once, until golden brown and puffed up. Check after about 6 minutes as they can easily catch. Serve at once.

Mustard and Parmesan cheese straws V

Cheese straws which aren't too fiddly! The mustard gives a lovely dark side to the straws too.

Makes about 40 straws (or 16 long ones)

1 x 375g (13 oz) packet ready-rolled puff pastry, approx. 35.5 x 23cm (14 x 9 in)	50g (2 oz) Parmesan, grated
2–3 tablespoons Dijon mustard	salt and freshly ground black pepper
	1 large egg, beaten

Preheat the oven to 220°C/425°F/Gas 7. Lightly grease 2 baking trays or line the trays with non-stick baking paper.

1 Unroll the pastry on a floured work surface and spread mustard over the top. Sprinkle evenly with Parmesan, salt and pepper. Cover with clingfilm and, using a rolling pin, roll the cheese into the pastry for a few minutes. Remove the clingfilm.

2 Divide the pastry in 4 widthways and cut each section into 10 strips about 1cm (½ in) thick for each straw. Twist each straw and place on the prepared baking trays. For extra-long cheese straws, cut the pastry in half widthways and divide each section into 8 strips, about 2.5cm (1 in) thick.

3 Glaze with the beaten egg and bake in the preheated oven for about 8–10 minutes (12 minutes for the long ones). Check the short straws after 5 minutes, the long after 8, to make sure they are not getting too brown. When the pastry is cooked through and golden brown, remove from the baking sheet and cool on a cooling rack.

cook now, eat later

TO PREPARE AND COOK AHEAD These can be made, cooked, cooled and then packed in a covered container and kept in the larder for 2–3 days. When storing, place between kitchen paper in a sealed container – this will stop them from becoming soggy. Refresh in the oven preheated to 200°C/400°F/Gas 6 for a few minutes to regain their crispness before serving.

TO FREEZE Cook, cool and freeze for up to 2 months. Thaw for about 15 minutes at room temperature. Refresh in the oven as above before serving.

TO COOK IN THE AGA Bake on the floor of the Roasting Oven for about 8 minutes, checking after 4 minutes. If the pastries are getting too brown, slide the cold sheet on to the second set of runners. When they are a perfect colour, transfer to the Simmering Oven to dry out.

Cocktail toad in the hole

Loved by both children and grown-ups! A wonderful way of using up leftover cocktail sausages.

Makes 36 'toads'

3 dozen cocktail pork sausages	250ml (8 fl oz) milk
100g (4 oz) plain flour	vegetable oil (optional)
2 eggs	creamed horseradish, mustard or mango
1 egg yolk	chutney (optional)

Preheat the oven to 220°C/425°F/Gas 7. You will need three 12-hole cocktail size tartlet tins.

1 Grill the sausages until completely cooked and golden brown (see above, or buy them ready cooked).

2 Measure the flour into a bowl, make a well in the centre of the flour and blend in the eggs and yolk with a little of the milk. Whisk to a smooth paste. Blend in the remaining milk to make a batter, and whisk really well until smooth.

3 Add a drop of oil (or fat from the sausages) to each tartlet tin. Slide the tins into the preheated oven to heat the fat. When the fat is smoking, drop a cooked sausage into the bottom of each tin and pour over the smooth batter. Return to the oven and bake for about 12–15 minutes until the batter is risen and golden brown. Check underneath one of the 'toads': it should be golden brown.

4 Spoon a tiny amount of horseradish, mustard or mango chutney on to each sausage before serving if liked. Allow to cool slightly, but serve warm.

cook now, eat later

TO PREPARE AND COOK AHEAD The sausages can be cooked up to 3 days ahead and kept in the fridge. The completed 'toads' can be made up to 14 hours ahead and reheated in the oven at 200°C/400°F/Gas 6 for about 5 minutes until hot right through.

TO FREEZE Not suitable.

TO COOK IN THE AGA Cook the sausages on non-stick paper in a roasting tin on the floor of the Roasting Oven until cooked and brown. Heat the oil on the second set of runners in the Roasting Oven and bake the 'toads' until well risen and golden brown, about 12–15 minutes. If reheating, do so in the Roasting Oven on the grid shelf on the floor for about 5 minutes until warmed through.

Home-made garlic herb cheese ^V

This cheese is so easy and yet so delicious, and, if you grow your own herbs, it is cheap too. Parsley, basil and chives are essential, but you can omit the others if preferred, or if they are unavailable.

Makes about 400g (14 oz)

a small bunch of fresh parsley

3 sprigs of fresh basil

2 sprigs of fresh thyme

1 sprig of fresh tarragon

a small bunch of fresh chives

about 350g (12 oz) rich cream cheese

1–2 small garlic cloves, crushed

a little single cream

salt and freshly ground black pepper

1 Take the stalks off the parsley and discard. Remove the leaves from the stems of the other herbs. Snip the chives finely.

2 Put the parsley, basil, thyme and tarragon leaves in a food processor and chop finely. Add the cheese and garlic, thin down with a little cream and season. Mix in the chives.

3 Serve on the cheese board or use for recipes. Good spread thinly on crostini.

cook now, eat later

TO PREPARE AHEAD

Prepare, cover and keep in the fridge for 2–3 days.

TO FREEZE Not suitable.

Peppadew and chèvre crostini ᵛ

Peppadew peppers can be bought in jars in good supermarkets.

Makes 20–25

about 2 tablespoons olive oil

1 garlic clove, crushed

a thin French stick/baguette

150g (5 oz) chèvre goat's cheese, in a roll

a little double cream

1 × 375g jar peppadew peppers

fresh basil leaves to garnish

Preheat the grill to its highest setting.

1 Mix together the oil and garlic in a small ramekin or bowl.

2 Thinly slice the baguette, and brush both sides with the garlic-flavoured olive oil. Place the bread on a small baking sheet which will fit under the grill, or line the grill pan with foil.

3 To cook the crostini, toast under the grill for about 2–3 minutes each side until pale golden brown and crisp. Watch them carefully. Cool on a wire rack.

4 Mash the chèvre (use the rind as well) with a little cream. Spread on to the cold crostini, keeping a little back. Drain and dry about 15 peppers, coarsely chop and arrange on the cheese. Dot the peppers with an additional piece of cheese.

5 Heat the crostini for about 5 minutes under the preheated hot grill. Garnish each crostini with a basil leaf.

cook now, eat later

TO PREPARE AND COOK AHEAD Prepare to step 4 up to 8 hours ahead. Cover with clingfilm and keep in the fridge until ready to cook. Flash under a hot grill for 5 minutes when guests arrive.

TO FREEZE The crostini bases can be made up to 2 months ahead and frozen. Leave at room temperature until defrosted.

TO COOK IN THE AGA To cook the crostini bases, bake on a solid baking sheet on the floor of the Roasting Oven for about 5–6 minutes until pale golden, turning half-way through the cooking time. Spread the cold crostini with the cheese and peppers and reheat on the second set of runners in the Roasting Oven for about 5 minutes until warm right through.

INDEX